SCALE AND CHORD BOOK 1

Five-Finger Scales and Chords

by Nancy and Randall Faber

This book belongs to: ______________________________

Online Support
Visit **pianoadventures.com/scales** to find online support for this book!

Production Coordinator: Jon Ophoff
Engraving: Dovetree Productions, Inc.

ISBN 978-1-61677-661-9

Table of Contents

Chart Your Progress

This chart will help you and your teacher track and celebrate each step of your progress in learning major and minor five-finger scales, chords, and cross-hand arpeggios. There are many ways to practice. So check or color a box each time you have completed that activity!

All the great composers, whether classical, jazz, or rock, use scales not only to improve their technique, but also to create their own melodies and harmonies. Now it's your turn! Have fun playing a scale with the teacher duet; then launch into an improvisation with your teacher.

Your teacher may not ask you to do every activity. But if you do, your piano ability will soar!

SECTION 1

Memorize

SECTION 2

Major Cross-Hand Arpeggios

	legato *f*-*p*	staccato *f*-*p*	spell the chord	by memory
C major...16				
G major 16				
D major 16				
A major...17				
E major...17				
B major...17				
F major 18				
B♭ major 18				
E♭ major 18				
A♭ major.......................................19				
D♭ major.......................................19				
G♭ (F♯) major................................19				

SECTION 3

Transposing 5-Finger Major Pieces

	C	G	D	A	E	B	F	B♭	E♭	A♭	D♭	F♯ G♭
Dudelsack (unknown composer) 20												
Waltzing (Nancy Faber) 20												
Gliding Rhythm (Ferdinand Beyer)....21												

SECTION 4

Minor 5-Finger Scales (Pentascales)

	legato *f*-*p*	staccato *f*-*p*	say letter names	by memory	do the improvisation
C minor 22					
G minor 22					
D minor 23					
A minor 23					
E minor...24					
B minor 24					
F minor...25					
B♭ minor.......................................25					
E♭ minor 26					
G♯ minor.......................................26					
C♯ minor 27					
F♯ minor 27					
Keyboard Diagrams 28					

Table of Contents

Progress Chart continued...

SECTION 5

SECTION 6

Transpose

Improvise

Note to Teacher

Hidden Powers for 5-Finger Scales

Playing 5-finger scales has significant value for early-level pianists, whether children, teens, or adults. Consider these tips for developing five core areas of musicianship.

Technique

- Develop a round hand shape and firm fingertips.
- Listen for steady rhythm playing hands-alone and hands-together.
- Listen for dynamic evenness playing hands-alone and hands-together.
- Listen for *forte/piano* dynamic contrast for the repeat.
- For hands-together, listen for precision of the fingers striking exactly at the same time.
- Recognize 1-3-5 thirds, blocked and broken.
- Play all twelve 5-finger scales chromatically up the keyboard: C, D♭, D, E♭, E, F, etc.
- Prepare the hand shifts by feeling the black keys.

Ear-Training

- Create short melodies within the 5-finger scale for student "play-back" or "sing-back."
- Create short melodies that end on step 1 (the tonic) or step 5 (the dominant). Student identifies the last note as the tonic ("home note") or the dominant ("active note").
- Explore musical Questions and Answers. Teacher creates a Question, student creates an Answer. Reverse roles!

Improvisation

- The 5-finger scale gives a "playing field" for creating within familiar limits. For each 5-finger scale, an improvisation idea is provided to inspire imagery, character, and tempo.
- While the teacher duet establishes meter and mood, the student can explore:
  long notes and short notes
  forte and *piano* sounds
  staccato and legato touches
  the use of rests
- A less confident student may begin using only whole notes, and then venture into more complex patterns.

Theory & Transposition

- Harmonize the 5-finger scale patterns with tonic and dominant notes and with I and V7 chords.
- Introduce transposition as a vital part of theory skill at the keyboard.
- Transpose not just to other keys, but also between major and minor modes.

Note-Naming

- Use a manuscript notebook for students to copy a 5-finger scale and name the notes they have written.
- Memorize the white/black key configurations of the major and minor triads. Can the student find patterns? For instance:
  C, F, and G major chords are white-white-white.
  D, E, and A major chords are white-black-white.
  D♭, E♭, and A♭ major chords are black-white-black.
  G♭, B♭, and B major chords are each unique.

How to Use this Book

Chart Your Progress

Use pages 2-5 to chart the student's progress through all major and minor 5-finger scales, primary chords, transposition of pieces, and exploration of improvisation in all 12 keys.

The sample below from the Progress Chart shows ways of using the 5-finger scale to build technique, theory skill, and creative "play" at the keyboard. A completely filled Progress Chart will be reason for celebration!

Major 5-Finger Scales (Pentascales)	legato *f-p*	staccato *f-p*	say letter names	by memory	do the improvisation
C major..8					
G major 8					

Teacher Duets

Each major and minor key has an engaging teacher duet (sample below) that is used for both the 5-finger scale exercise and the improvisation to follow. Link technique and creativity by performing the scale exercise, then immediately going into the improvisation.

Teacher Duet: (Student plays *1 octave higher*, then improvises)

Order of Keys

Teachers may teach the order of major and minor 5-finger scales as presented or use their own program. Keep track of progress by using the chart at the front of the book (pages 2-5).

C	G	D	A	E	B	F	B♭	E♭	A♭	D♭	F♯ G♭

Online Support

Download theory pages for practice in writing major and minor 5-finger scales. Visit **pianoadventures.com/scales**

SECTION 1

Major 5-Finger Scales

C Major

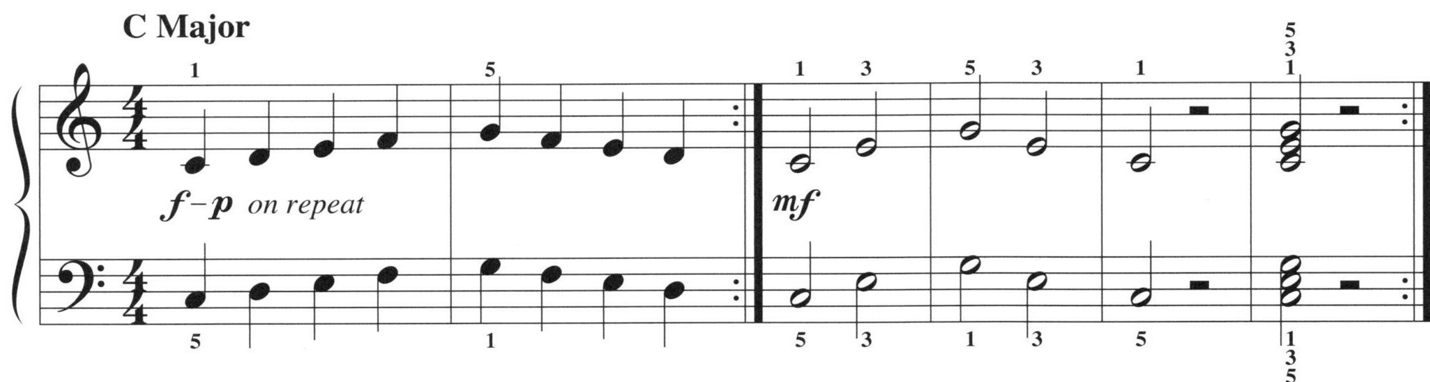

Teacher Duet: (Student plays *1 octave higher*, then improvises)

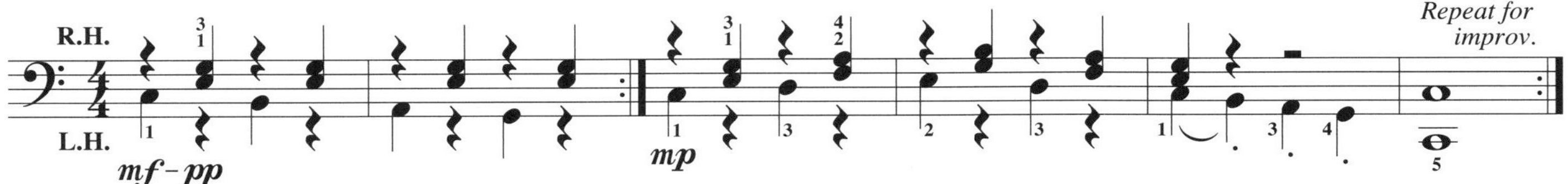

legato f-p	staccato f-p	say letter names	by memory	do the improvisation

Improvise!

- A happy march.
- Include repeated notes and *staccato* notes.

G Major

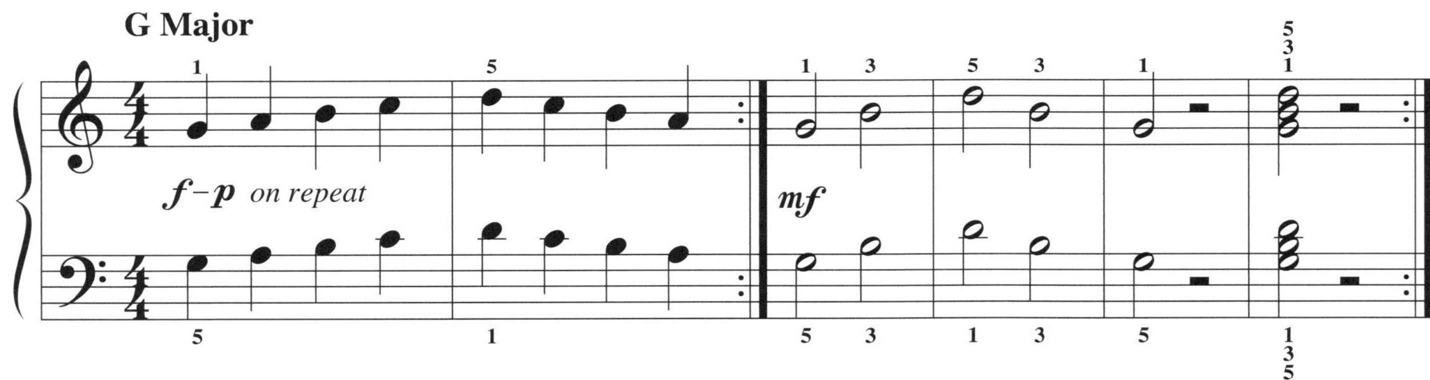

Teacher Duet: (Student plays *1 octave higher*, then improvises)

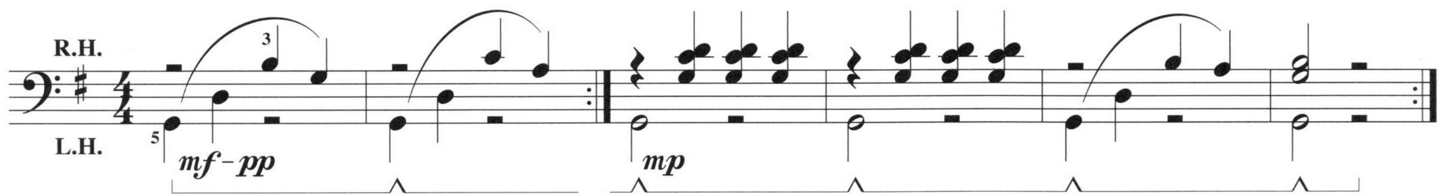

legato f-p	staccato f-p	say letter names	by memory	do the improvisation

Improvise!

- Imagine a starry night.
- Play *legato* and use long notes.

D Major

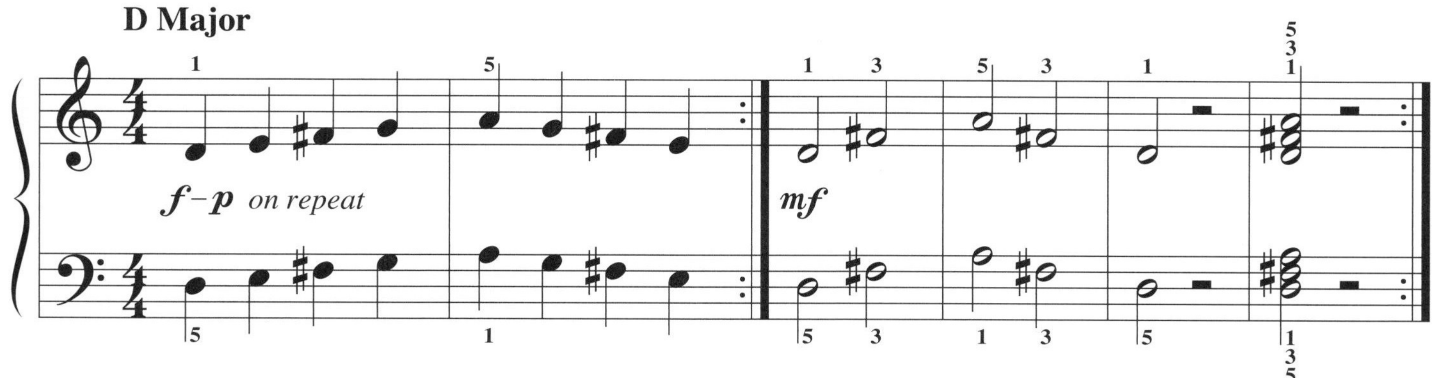

Teacher Duet: (Student plays *1 octave higher*, then improvises)

legato *f - p*	staccato *f - p*	say letter names	by memory	do the improvisation

Improvise!

- Imagine a gliding boat.
- Include a *forte* and *piano* echo.

A Major

Teacher Duet: (Student plays *1 octave higher*, then improvises)

legato *f - p*	staccato *f - p*	say letter names	by memory	do the improvisation

Improvise!

- Think of a jazz band.
- Make up some jazzy, swing rhythms!

E Major

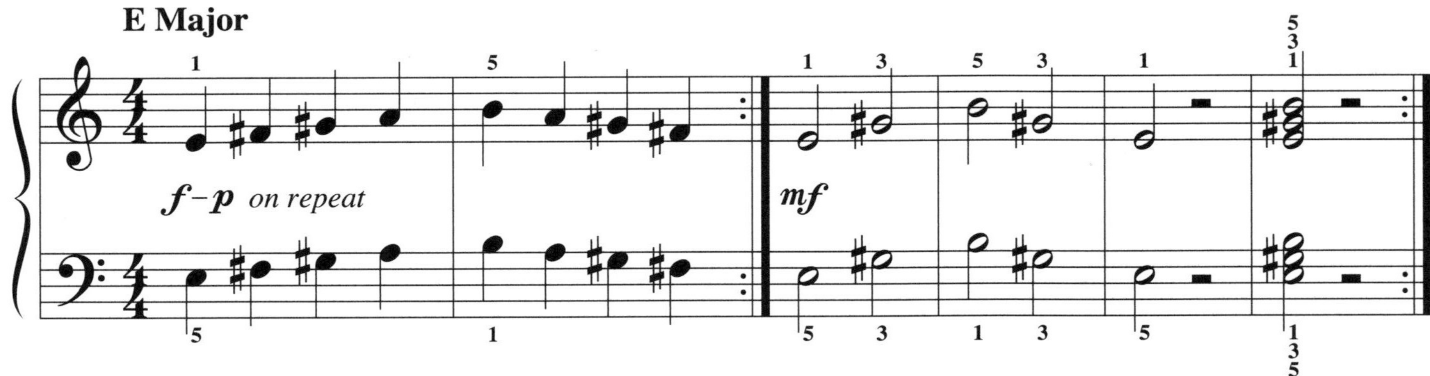

Teacher Duet: (Student plays *1 octave higher*, then improvises)

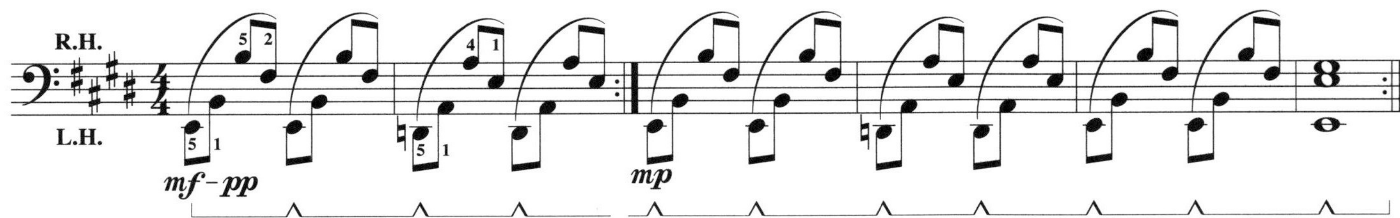

legato *f-p*	staccato *f-p*	say letter names	by memory	do the improvisation

Improvise!

- Imagine daydreaming on a cloudy day.
- Include an octave shift.

B Major

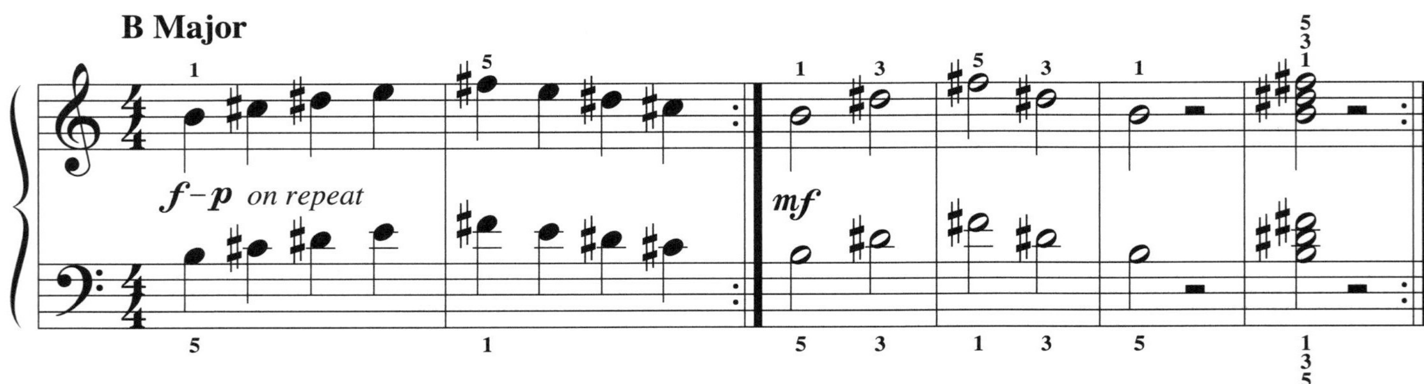

Teacher Duet: (Student plays *1 octave higher*, then improvises)

legato *f-p*	staccato *f-p*	say letter names	by memory	do the improvisation

Improvise!

- Create a hero's march.
- Can you play in parallel motion?

F Major

Teacher Duet: **(Student plays *1 octave higher*, then improvises)**

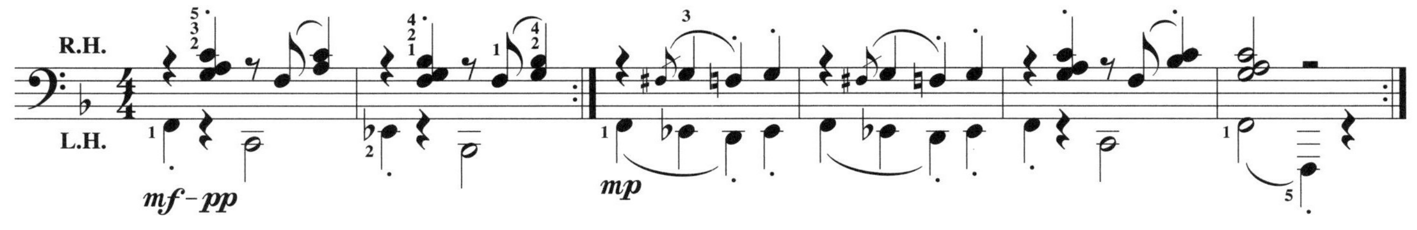

legato *f-p*	staccato *f-p*	say letter names	by memory	do the improvisation

Improvise!

- Imagine hiking on a sunny day.
- Include an F major broken chord.

B♭ Major

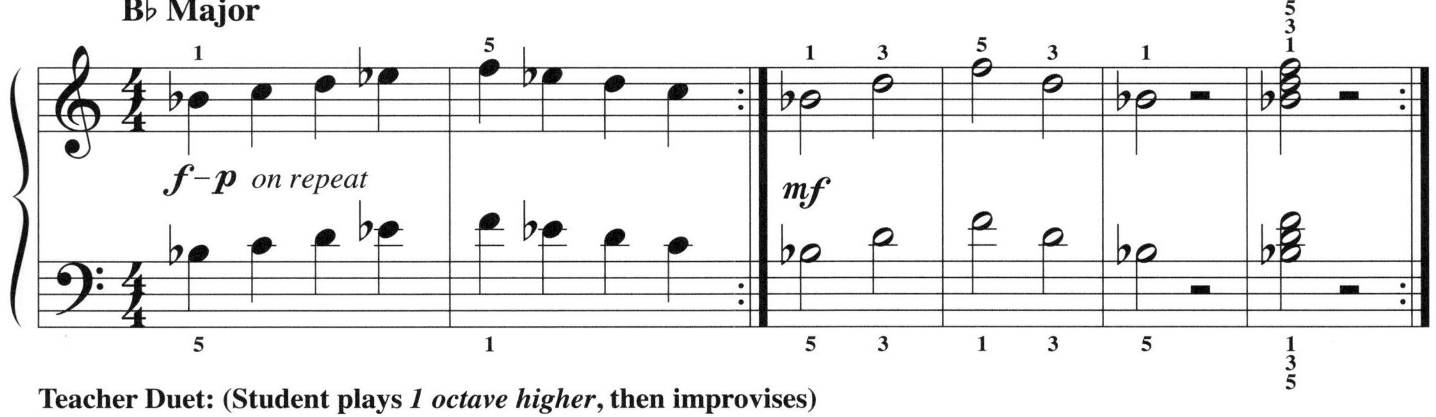

Teacher Duet: **(Student plays *1 octave higher*, then improvises)**

legato *f-p*	staccato *f-p*	say letter names	by memory	do the improvisation

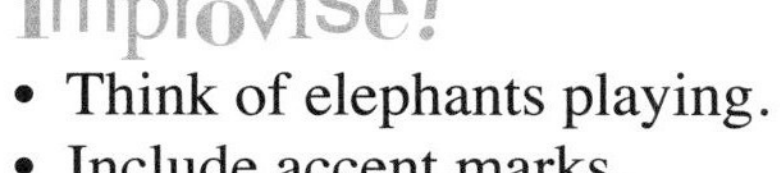

- Think of elephants playing.
- Include accent marks.

E♭ Major

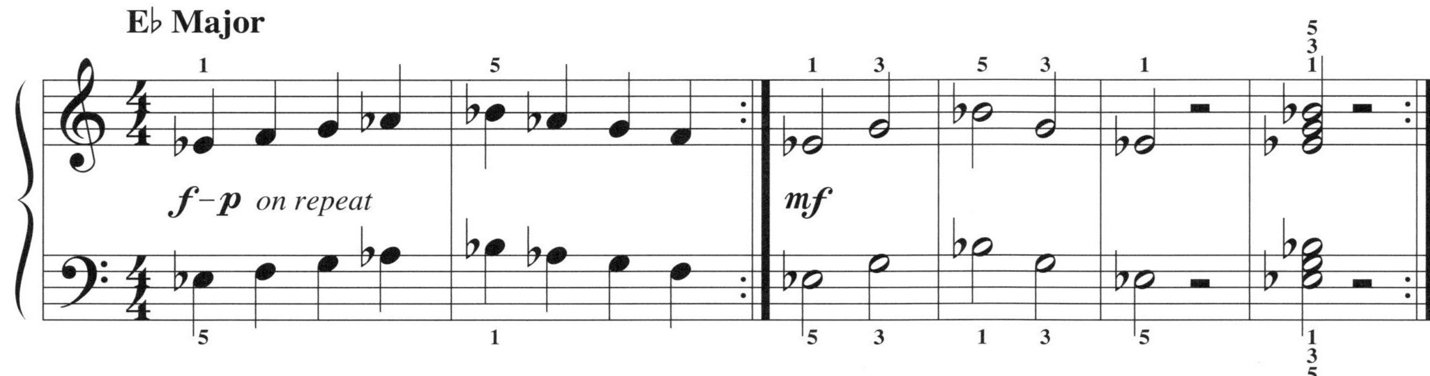

Teacher Duet: (Student plays *1 octave higher*, then improvises)

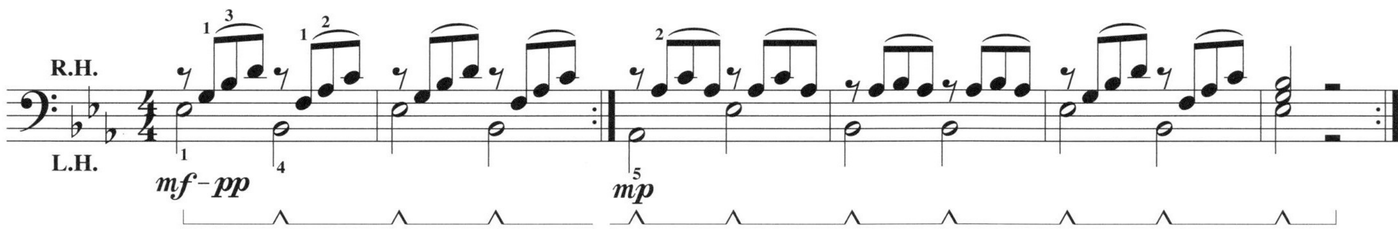

legato *f-p*	staccato *f-p*	say letter names	by memory	do the improvisation

Improvise!

- Think of canoeing in the moonlight.
- Include very long notes.

A♭ Major

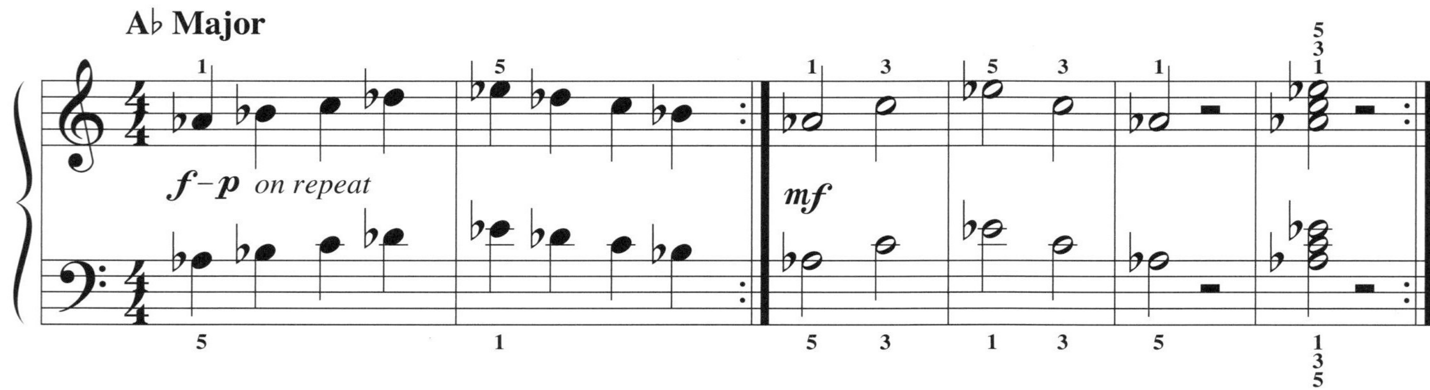

Teacher Duet: (Student plays *1 octave higher*, then improvises)

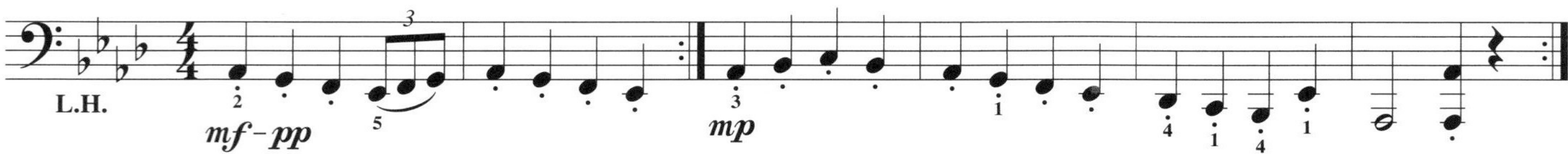

legato *f-p*	staccato *f-p*	say letter names	by memory	do the improvisation

Improvise!

- Think of a tuba in a band.
- Include *staccato* sounds and rests.

D♭ Major

legato f-p	staccato f-p	say letter names	by memory	do the improvisation

Improvise!

- Imagine a soccer game.
- Include 4ths and 5ths.

G♭ Major

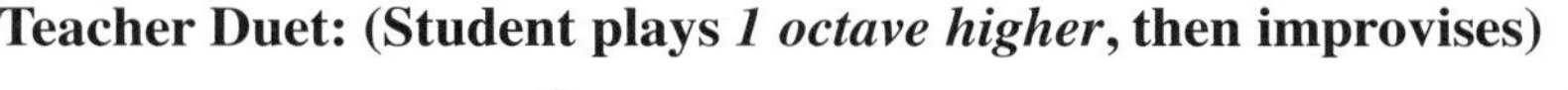

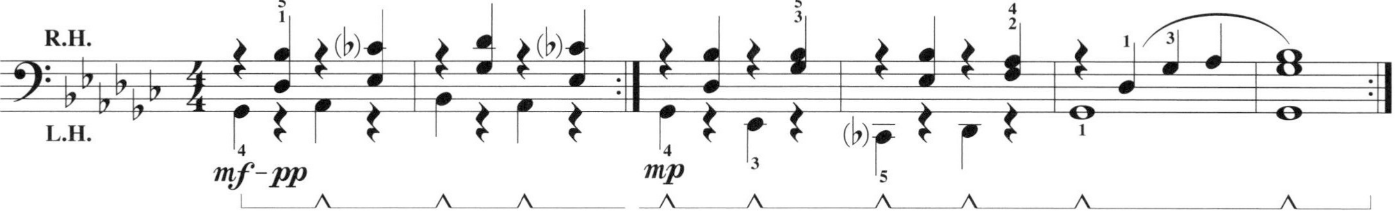

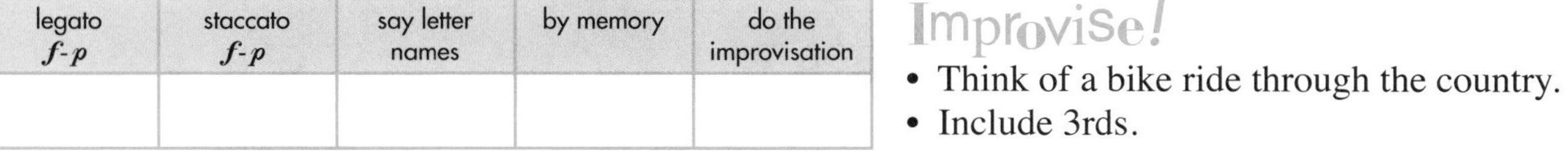

legato f-p	staccato f-p	say letter names	by memory	do the improvisation

Improvise!

- Think of a bike ride through the country.
- Include 3rds.

also written as F♯ Major

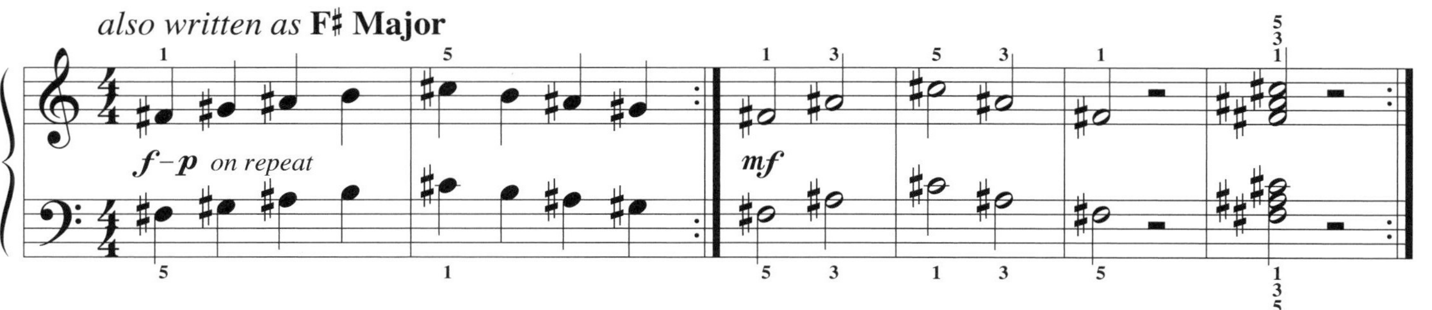

Keyboards for 5-Finger Major Scales

C Major

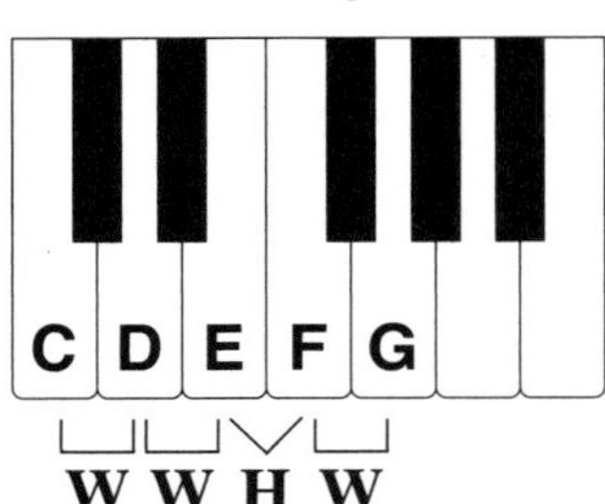

G Major

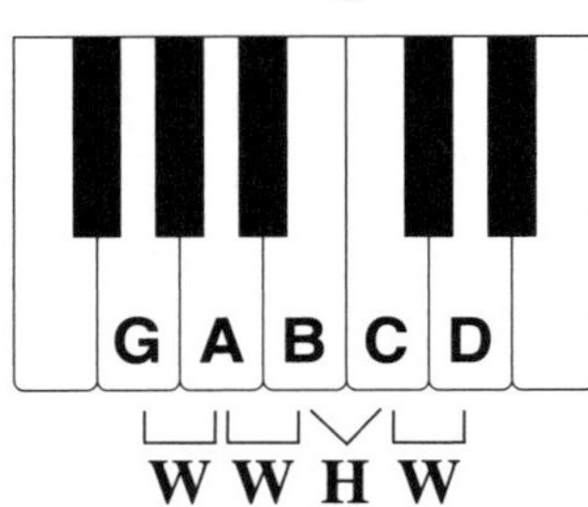

D Major

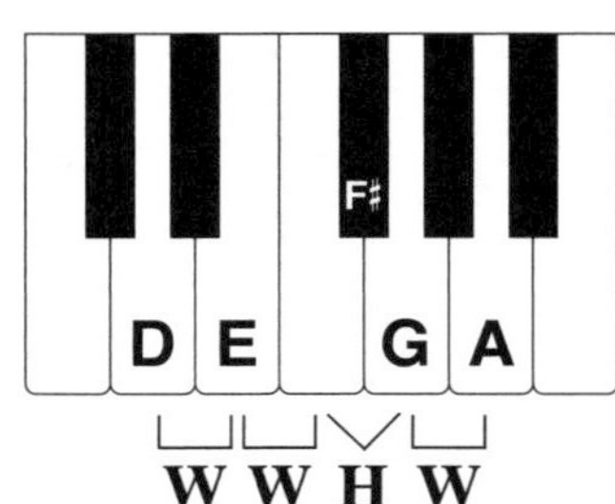

A Major

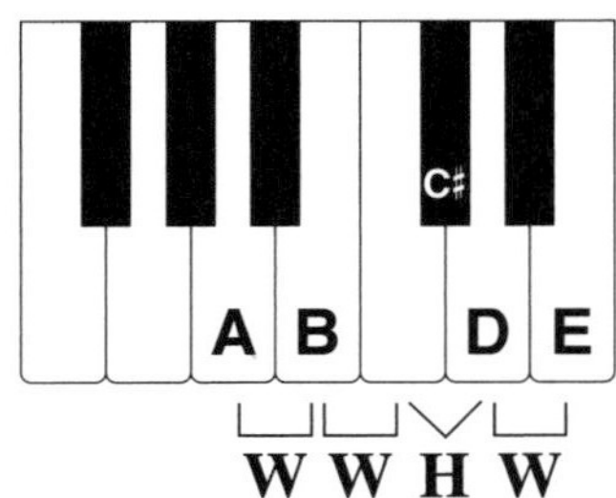

E Major

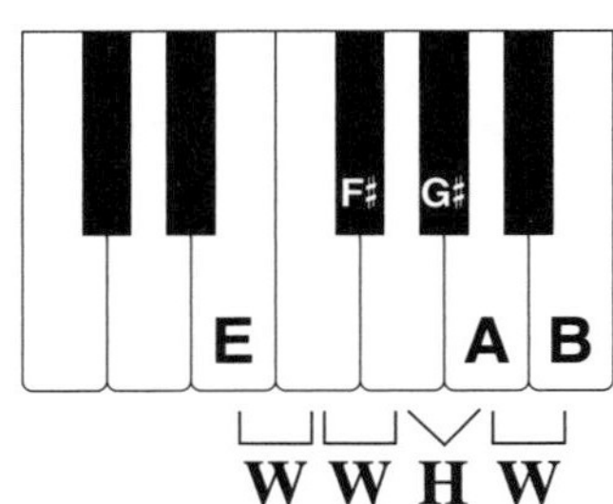

B Major

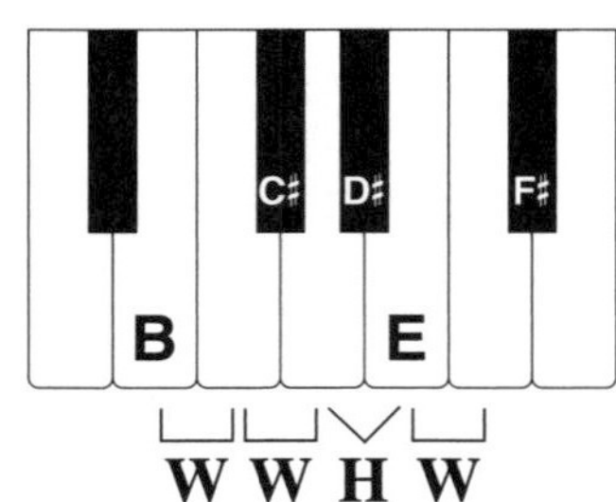

F Major

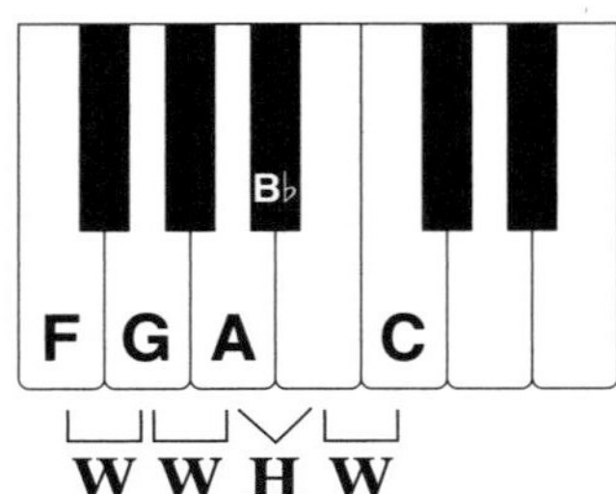

B♭ Major

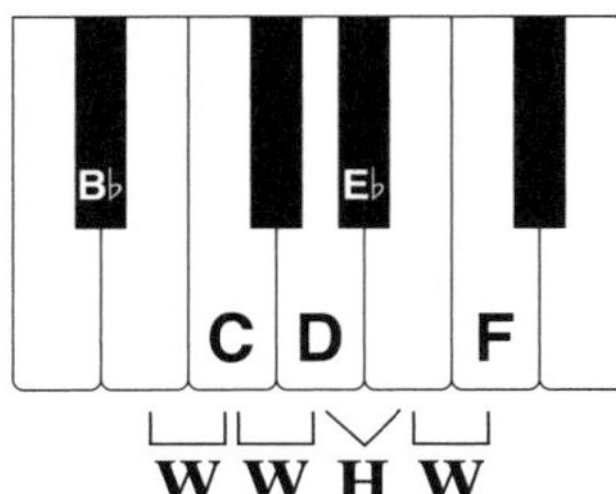

E♭ Major

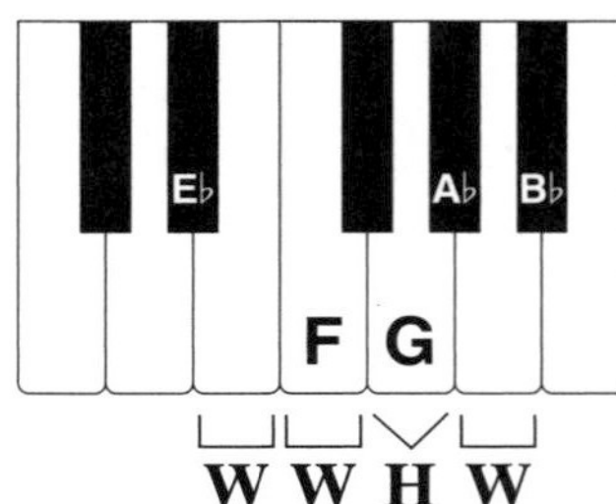

A♭ Major

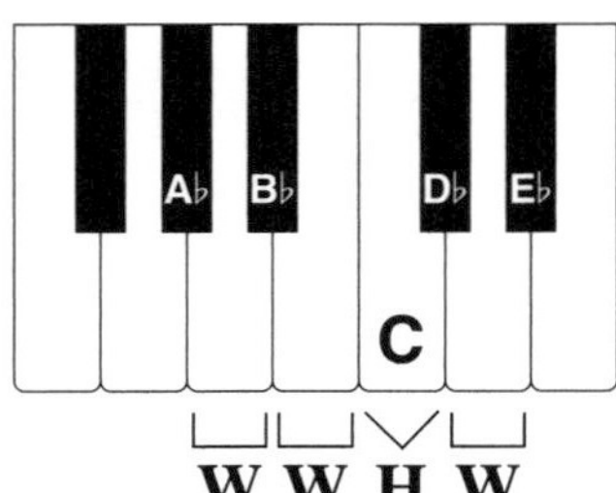

D♭ Major

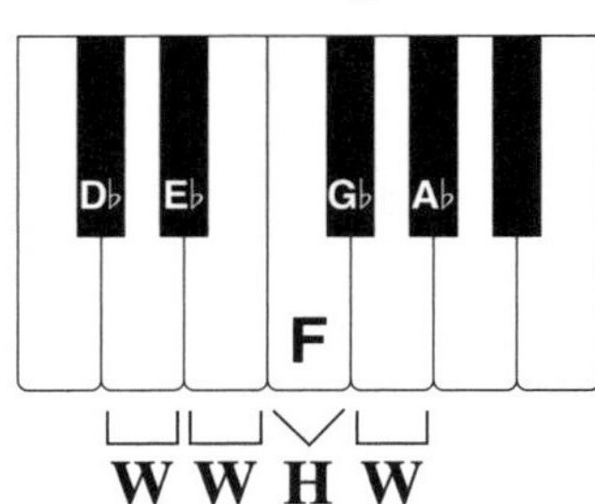

G♭ Major

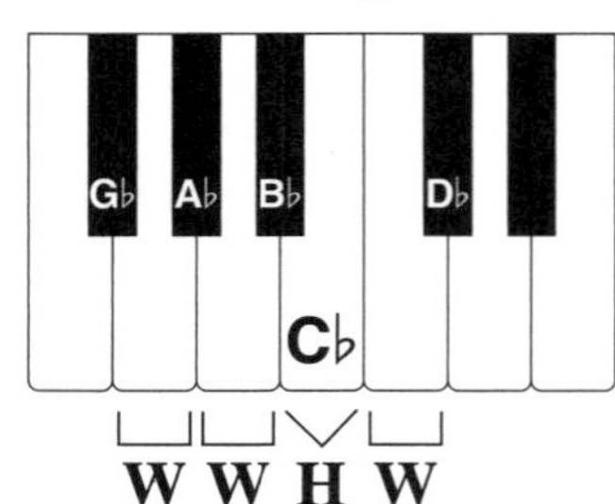

also written as

F♯ Major

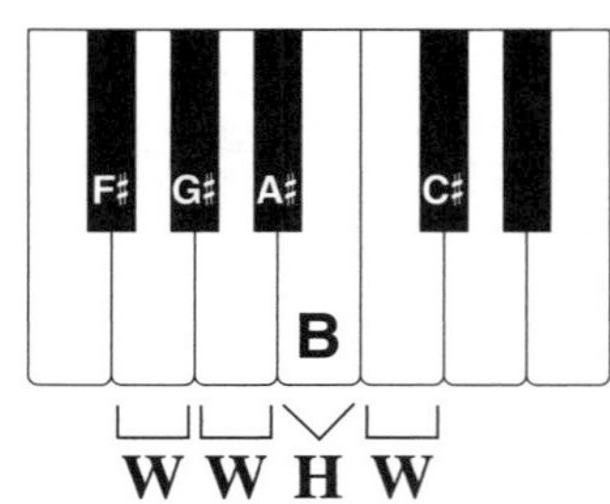

Your Turn!

Write the letter names of each major 5-finger scale on the keyboard given.

Mark the **whole** steps, ⌴, and **half** steps, ∨, as shown on page 14.

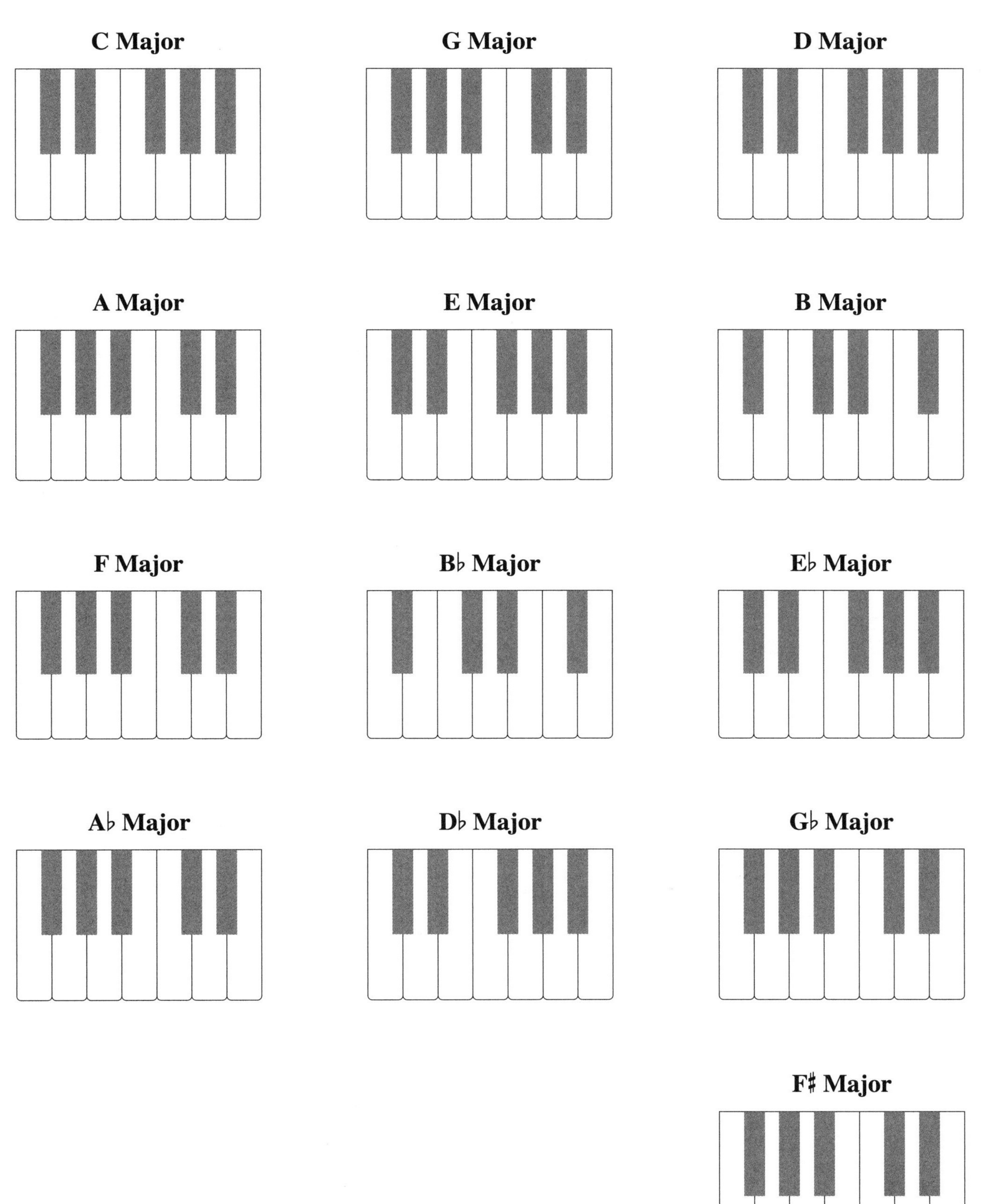

SECTION 2

Major Cross-Hand Arpeggios

After learning these well, your teacher may have you use the damper pedal.

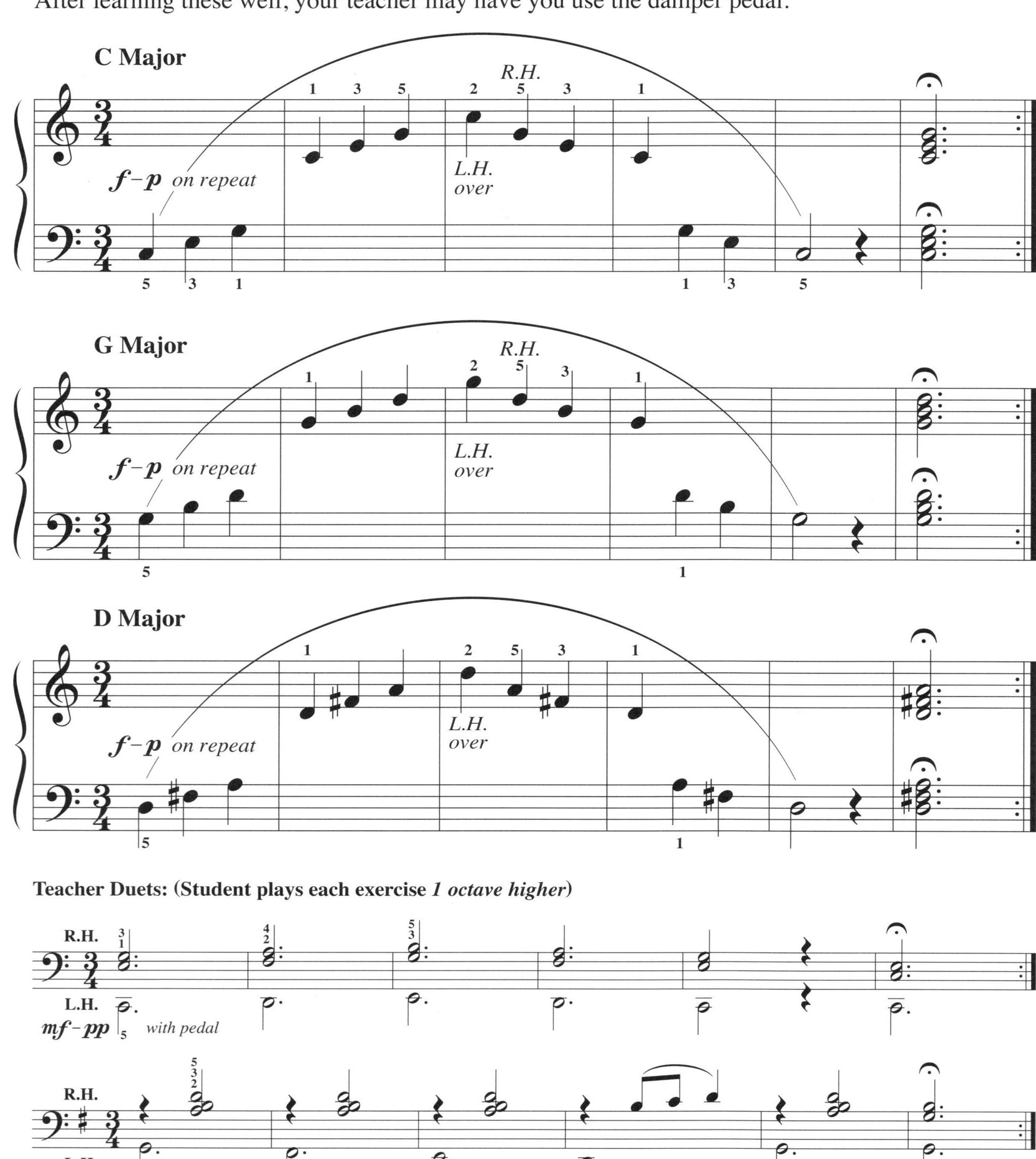

A Major
f–p on repeat
L.H. over
E Major
f–p on repeat
L.H. over
B Major
f–p on repeat
L.H. over
Teacher Duets: (Student plays each exercise 1 octave higher)
R.H.
L.H.
mf–pp with pedal
R.H.
L.H.
mf–pp with pedal
R.H.
L.H. mf–pp with pedal

F Major
1
2
f–p on repeat
L.H.
over
5
B♭ Major
1
2
f–p on repeat
L.H.
over
5
E♭ Major
1
2
f–p on repeat
L.H.
over
5
Teacher Duets: (Student plays each exercise 1 octave higher)
R.H.
L.H.
mf–pp
with pedal
4
2
(no pedal)
5
1
5
with pedal

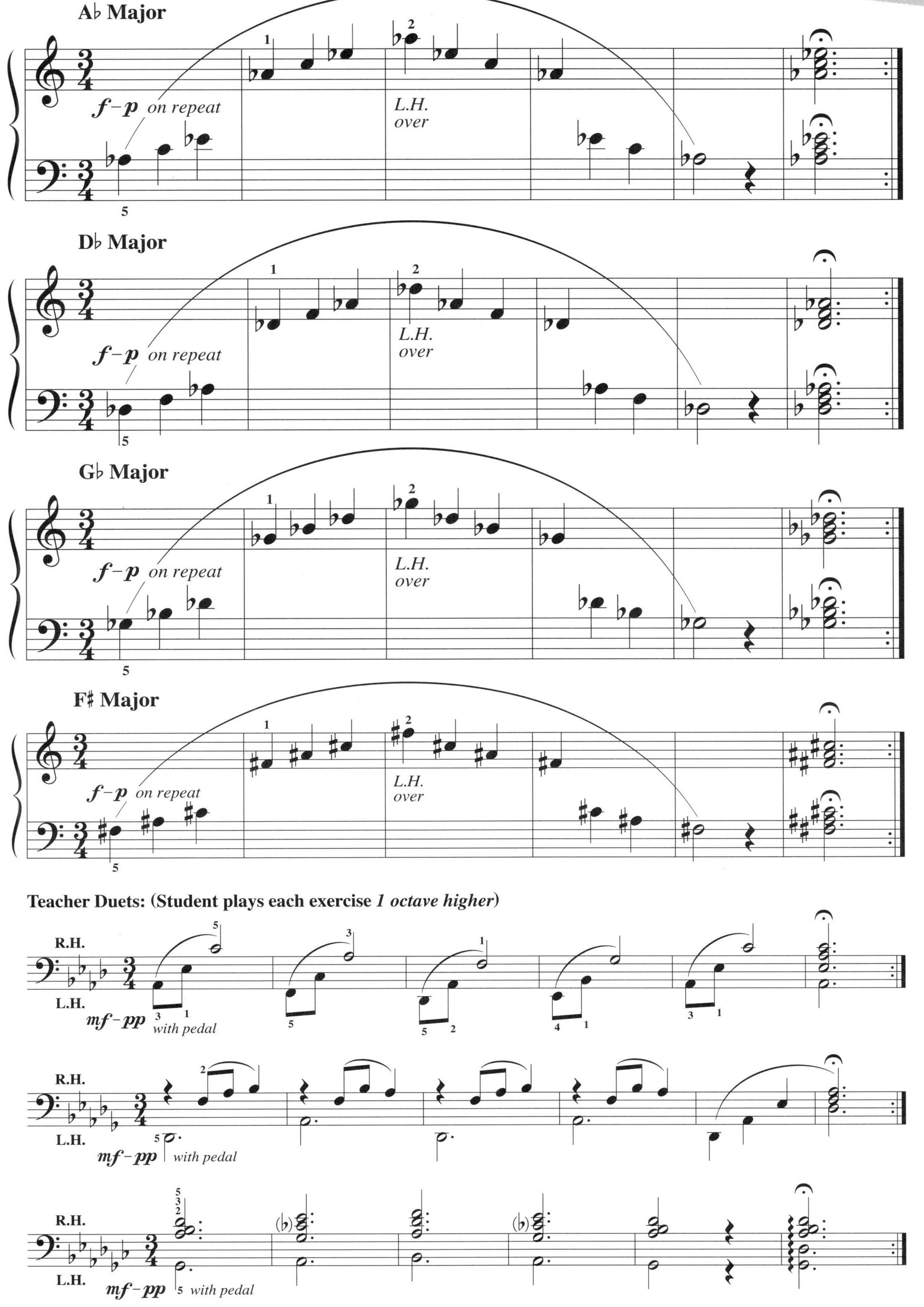
A♭ Major
f–p on repeat
L.H. over
D♭ Major
f–p on repeat
L.H. over
G♭ Major
f–p on repeat
L.H. over
F♯ Major
f–p on repeat
L.H. over
Teacher Duets: (Student plays each exercise 1 octave higher)
R.H.
L.H.
mf–pp with pedal
R.H.
L.H.
mf–pp with pedal
R.H.
L.H.
mf–pp with pedal

Transposing 5-Finger Major Pieces

Dudelsack

___ Major 5-Finger Scale

Unknown composer (ca. 1600)

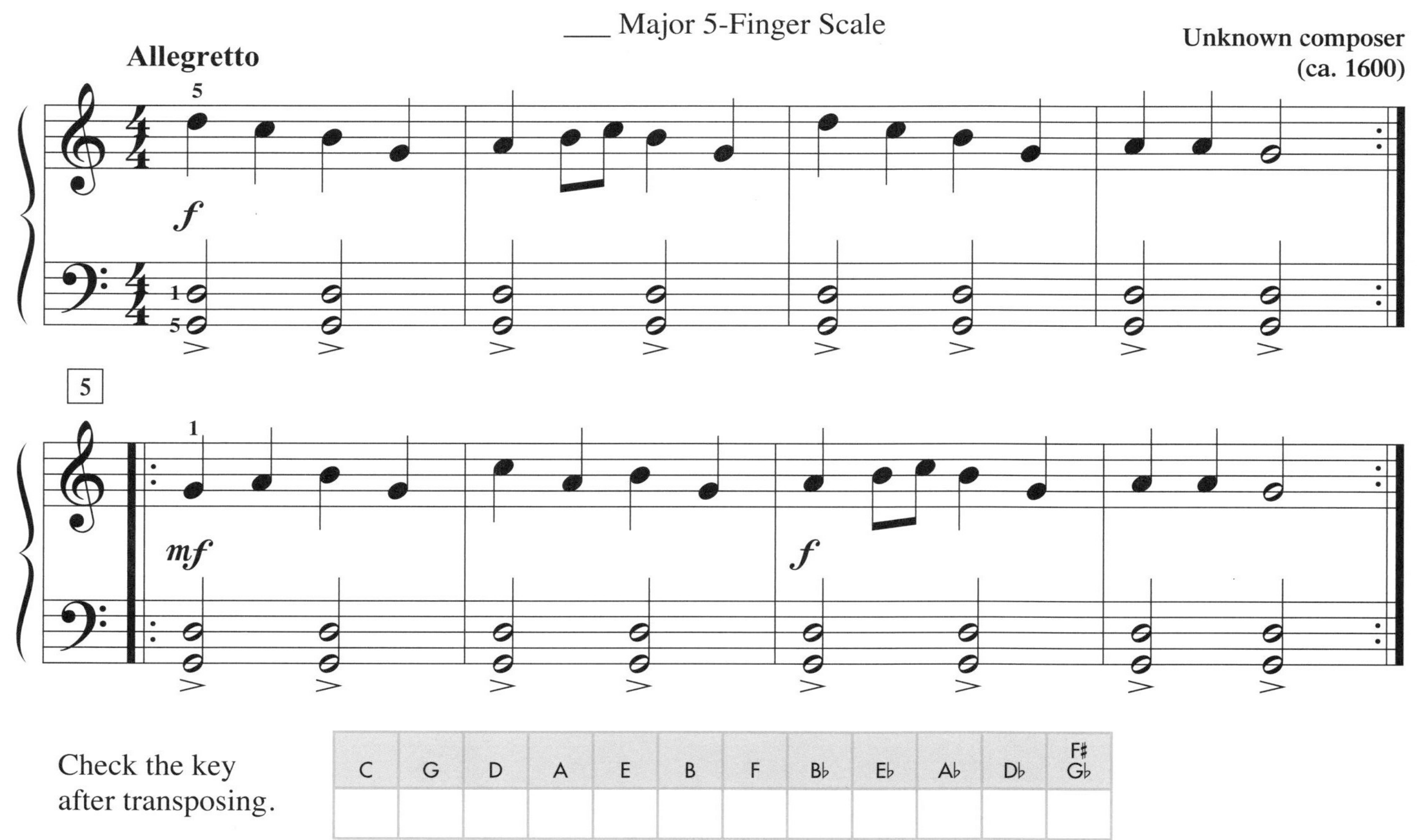

Check the key after transposing.

C	G	D	A	E	B	F	B♭	E♭	A♭	D♭	F♯ G♭

Waltzing

___ Major 5-Finger Scale

Nancy Faber (b. 1955)

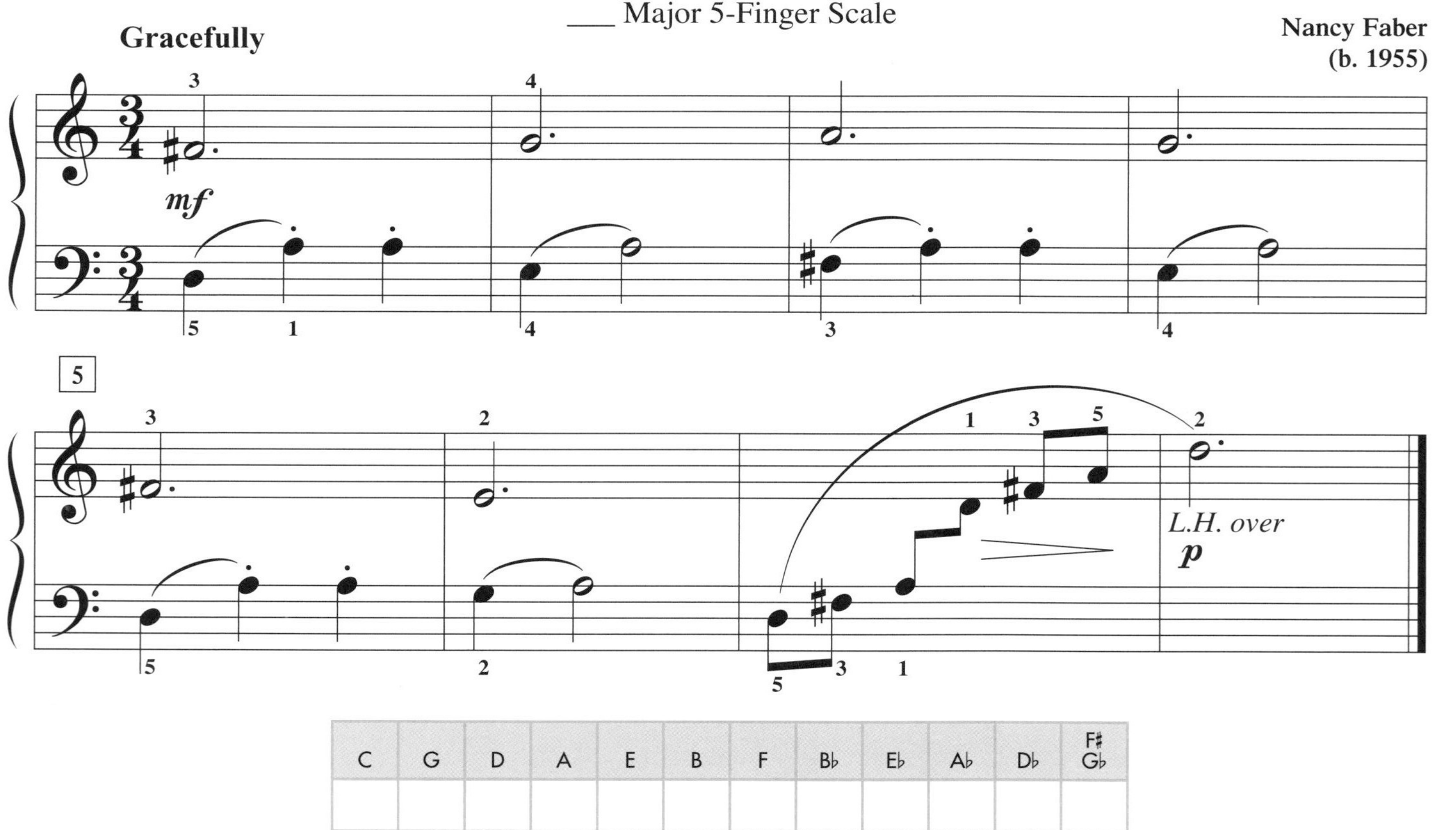

C	G	D	A	E	B	F	B♭	E♭	A♭	D♭	F♯ G♭

Gliding Rhythm

from Opus 101*

___ Major 5-Finger Scale

C	G	D	A	E	B	F	B♭	E♭	A♭	D♭	F♯ G♭

*Originally for right hand only.

Minor 5-Finger Scales

C minor

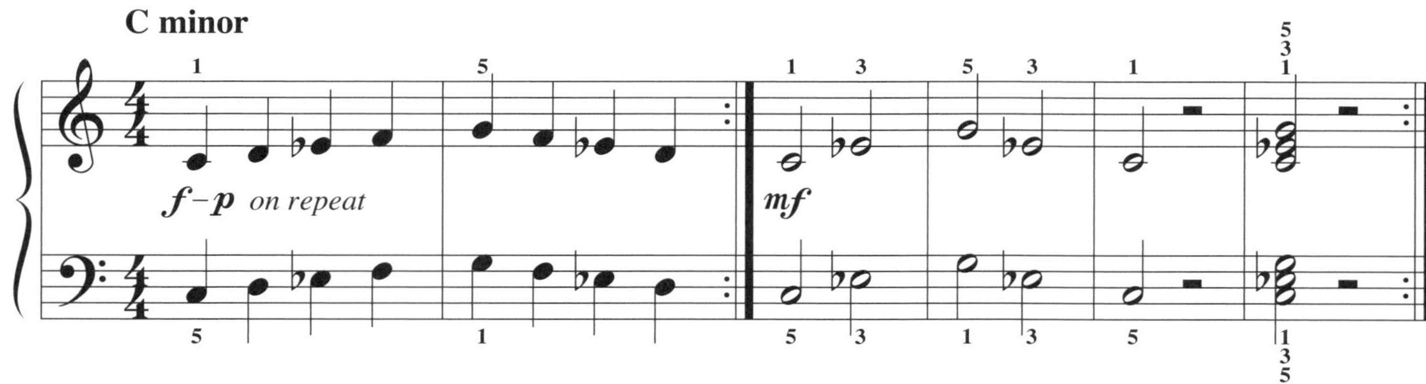

Teacher Duet: (Student plays *1 octave higher*, then improvises)

legato *f-p*	staccato *f-p*	say letter names	by memory	do the improvisation

Improvise!

- Think of trolls marching along.
- Include lots of *forte* E-flats.

G minor

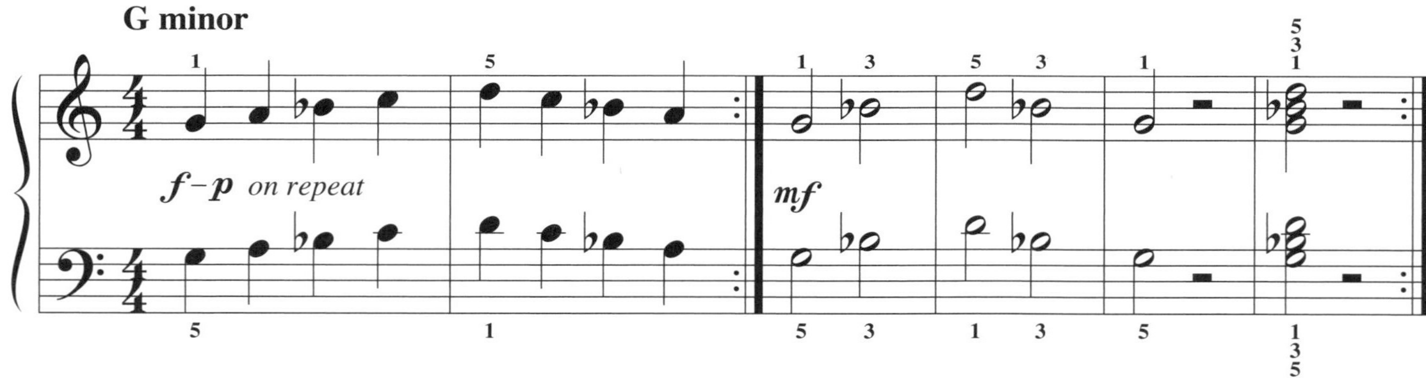

Teacher Duet: (Student plays *1 octave higher*, then improvises)

legato *f-p*	staccato *f-p*	say letter names	by memory	do the improvisation

Improvise!

- Think of pirates dancing on a ship.
- Include G minor chords.

D minor

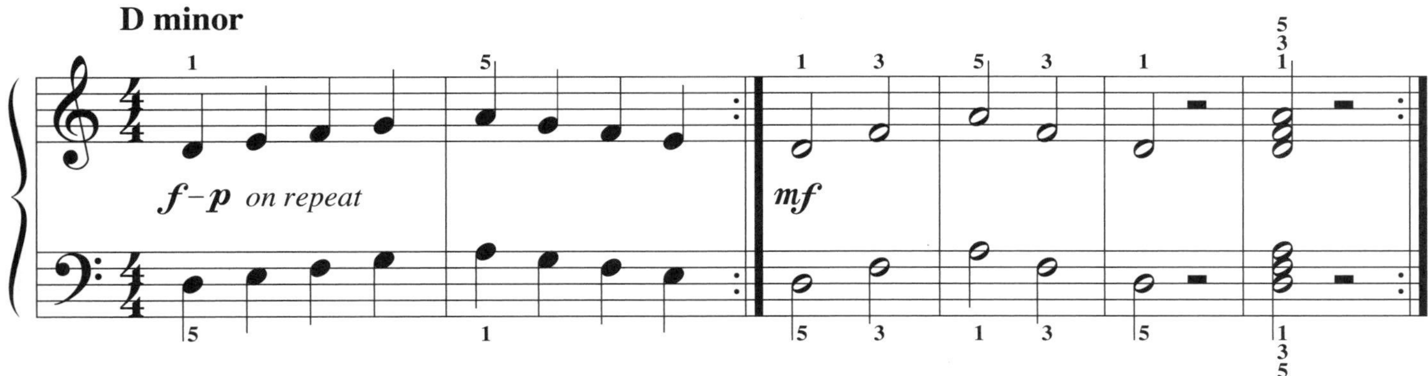

Teacher Duet: (Student plays *1 octave higher*, then improvises)

legato *f-p*	staccato *f-p*	say letter names	by memory	do the improvisation

Improvise!

- Think of a magician pulling a rabbit out of a hat.
- Include rests.

A minor

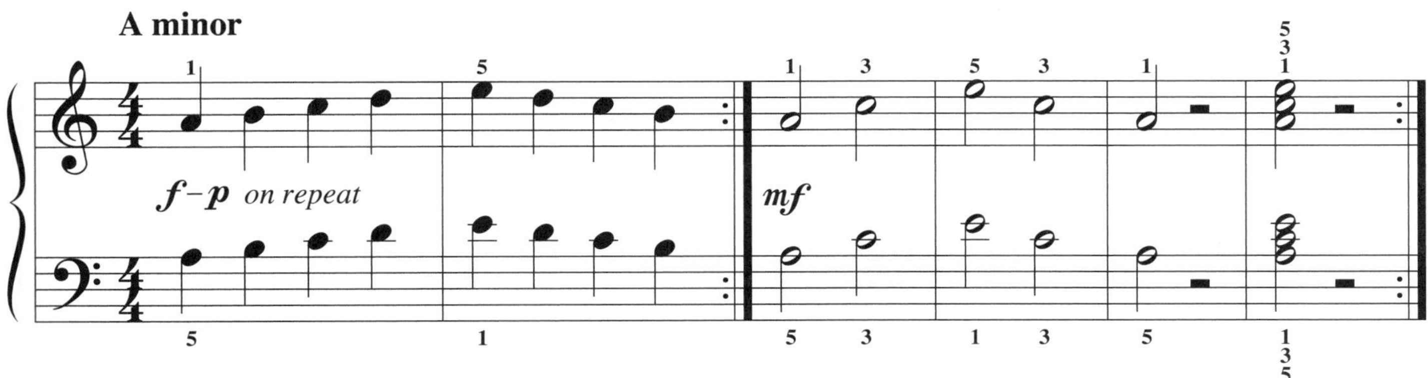

Teacher Duet: (Student plays *1 octave higher*, then improvises)

legato *f-p*	staccato *f-p*	say letter names	by memory	do the improvisation

Improvise!

- Think of a pep band at the football game.
- Include hands-together unison playing.

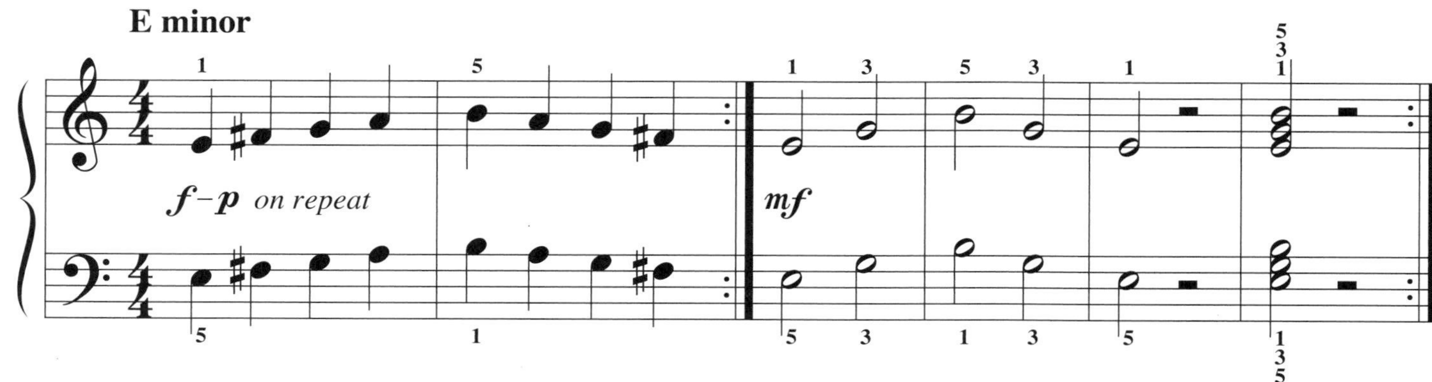

Teacher Duet: (Student plays *1 octave higher*, then improvises)

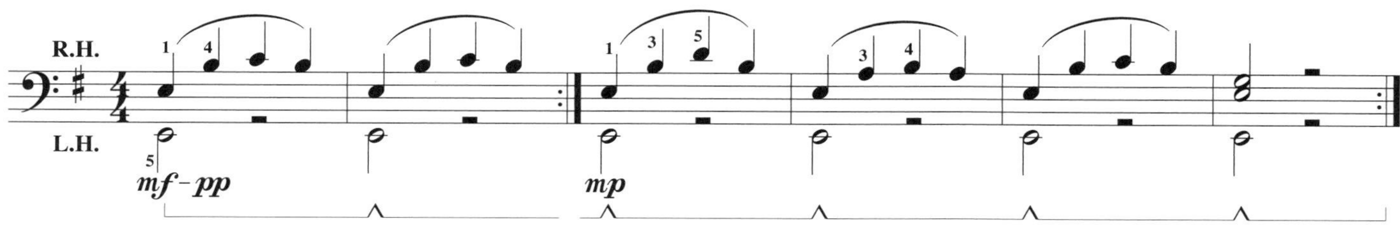

legato *f-p*	staccato *f-p*	say letter names	by memory	do the improvisation

Improvise!

- Think of mist rolling in from the sea.
- Include *piano* sounds and long tones.

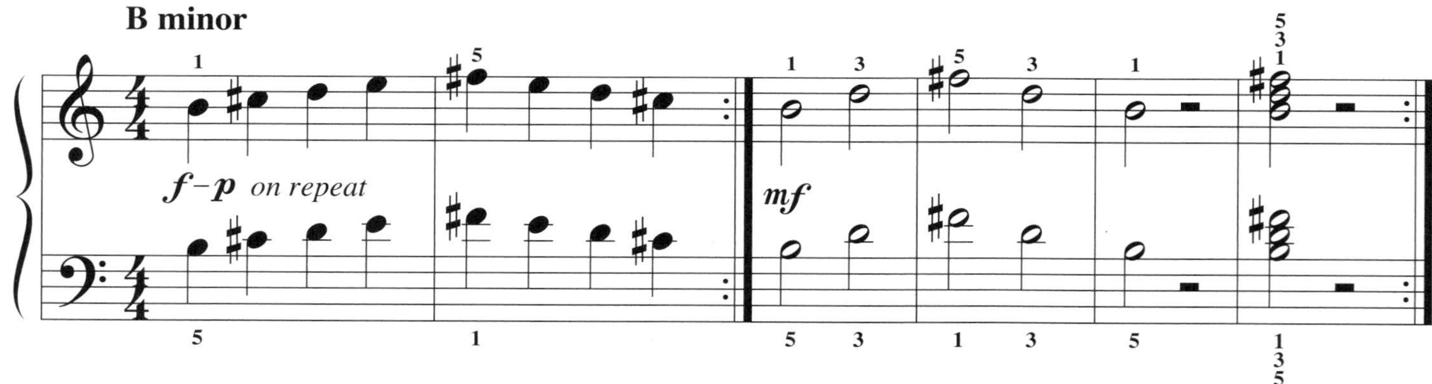

Teacher Duet: (Student plays *1 octave higher*, then improvises)

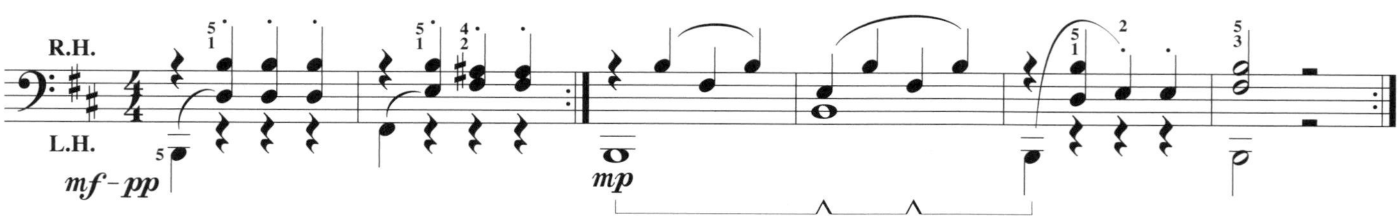

legato *f-p*	staccato *f-p*	say letter names	by memory	do the improvisation

Improvise!

- Think of a busy traffic jam.
- Include short bursts of sound.

F minor

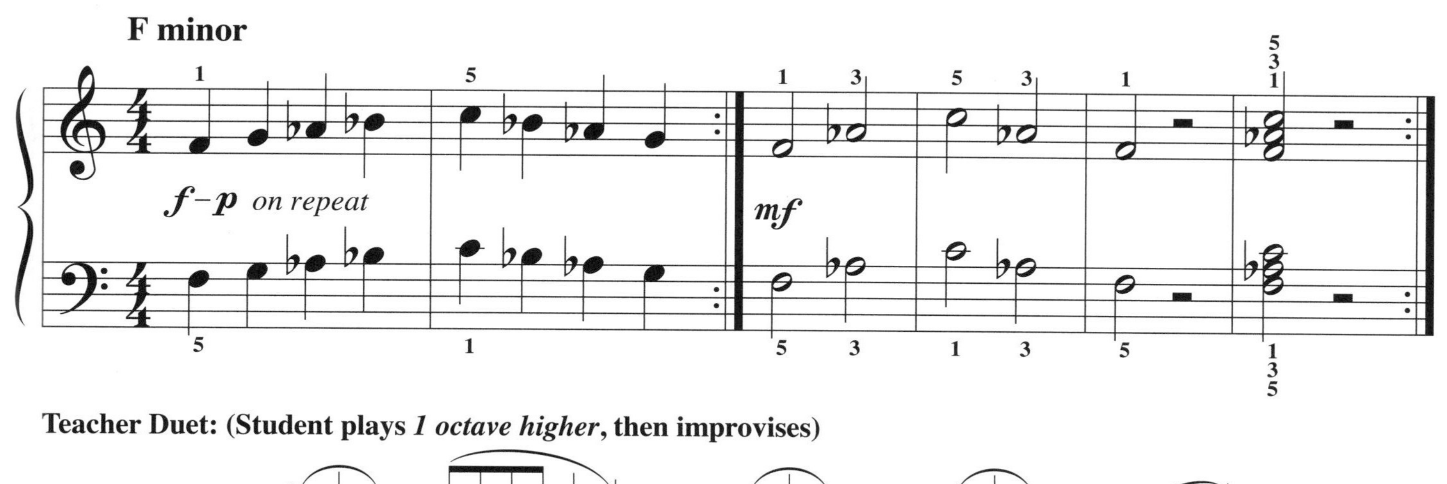

Teacher Duet: (Student plays *1 octave higher*, then improvises)

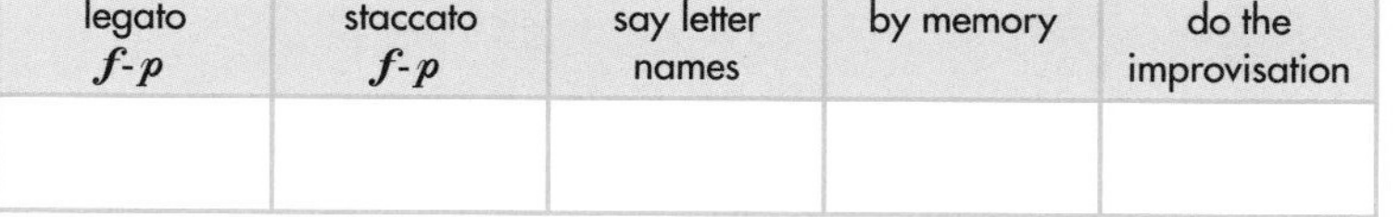

legato f-p	staccato f-p	say letter names	by memory	do the improvisation

Improvise!

- Think of fall leaves blowing.
- Include broken F minor chords.

B♭ minor

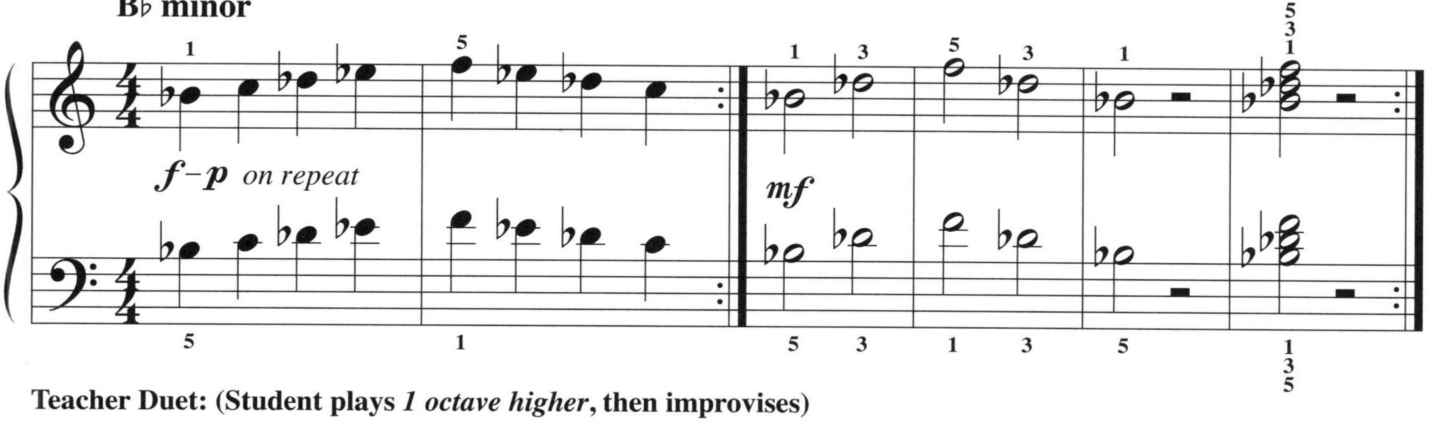

Teacher Duet: (Student plays *1 octave higher*, then improvises)

legato f-p	staccato f-p	say letter names	by memory	do the improvisation

Improvise!

- Think of horses strutting.
- Include *staccato* sounds.

E♭ minor

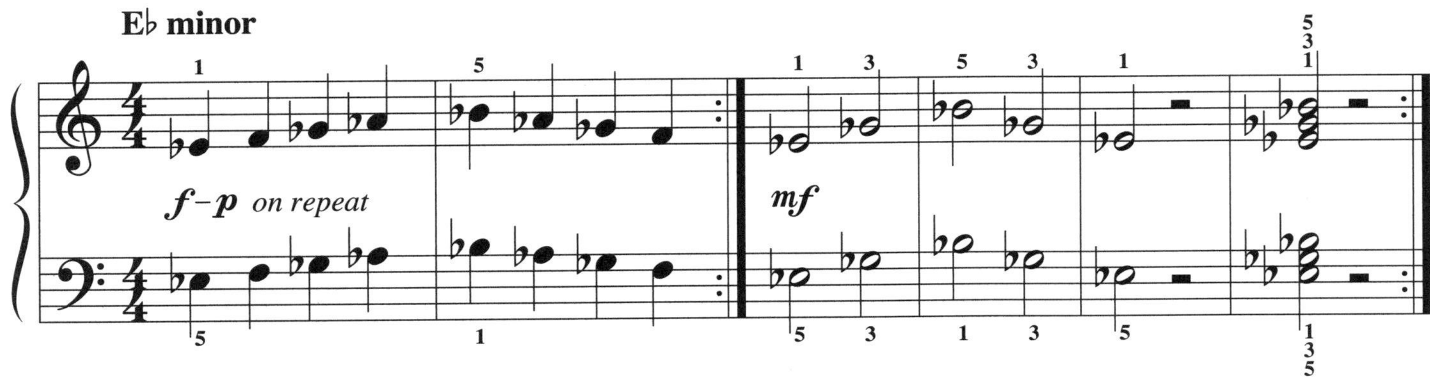

Teacher Duet: (Student plays *1 octave higher*, then improvises)

legato *f-p*	staccato *f-p*	say letter names	by memory	do the improvisation

Improvise!

- Think of gathering storm clouds.
- Include blocked E♭ minor chords.

G♯ minor

Teacher Duet: (Student plays *1 octave higher*, then improvises)

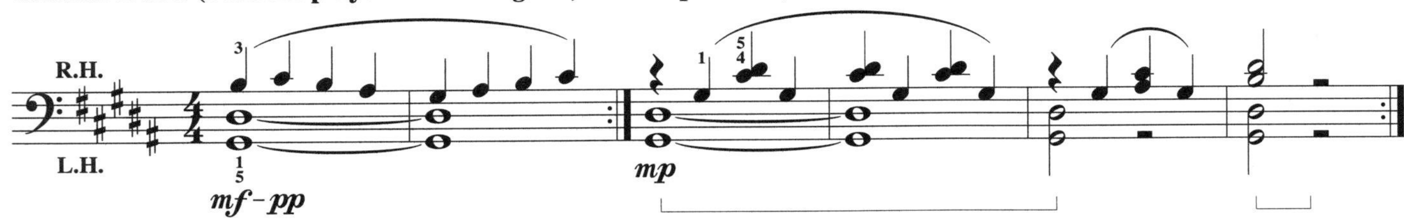

legato *f-p*	staccato *f-p*	say letter names	by memory	do the improvisation

Improvise!

- Think of a gypsy tale by the fire.
- Include blocked G♯ minor chords.

C♯ minor

Teacher Duet: (Student plays *1 octave higher*, then improvises)

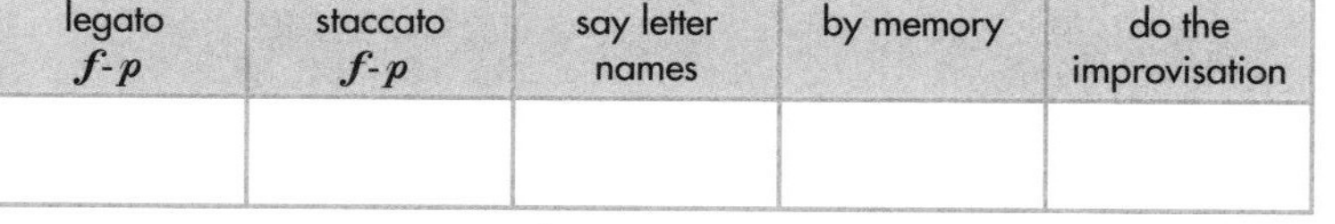

legato *f-p*	staccato *f-p*	say letter names	by memory	do the improvisation

Improvise!

- Think of a boogie-woogie band.
- Include jazzy rhythms.

F♯ minor

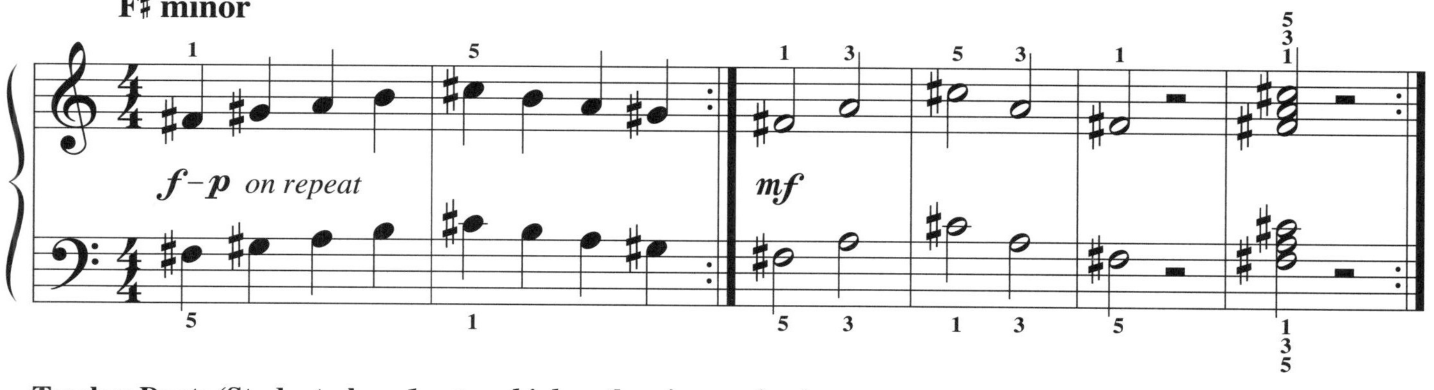

Teacher Duet: (Student plays *1 octave higher*, then improvises)

legato *f-p*	staccato *f-p*	say letter names	by memory	do the improvisation

Improvise!

- Think of riding a camel in the desert.
- Include a short idea that you repeat.

Keyboards for 5-finger Minor Scales

C minor

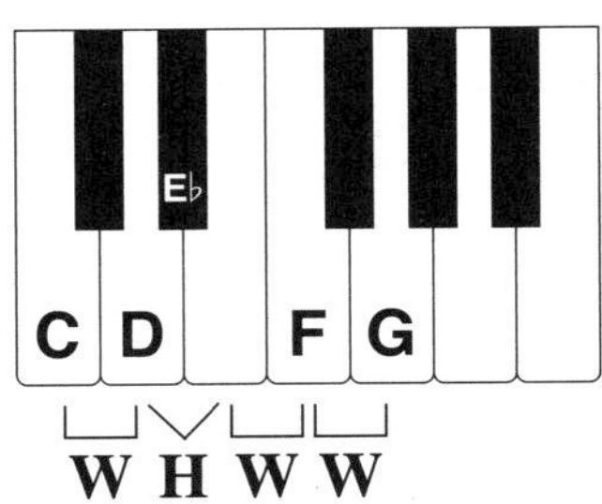

G minor

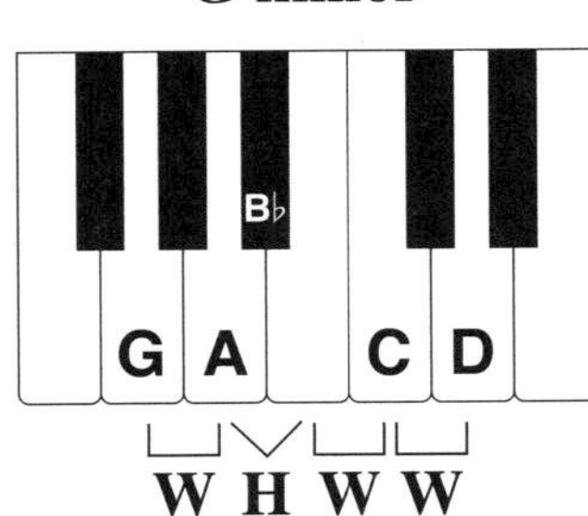

D minor

A minor

E minor

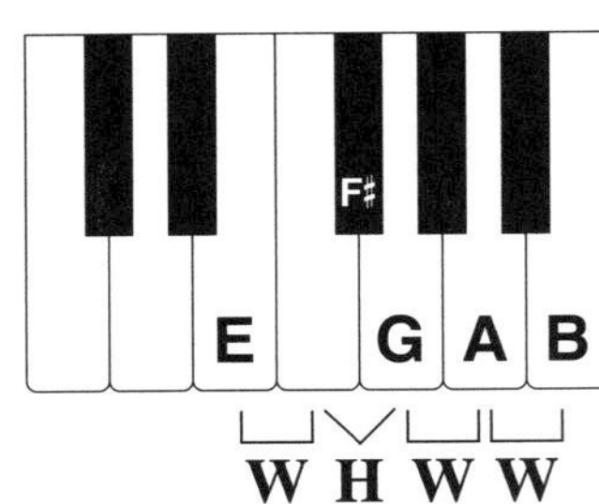

B minor

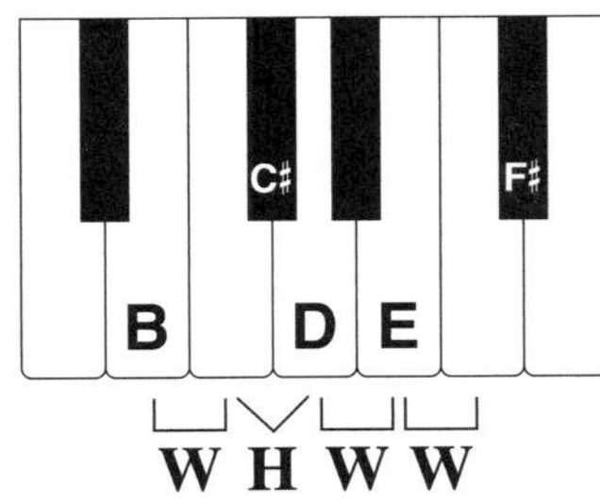

F minor

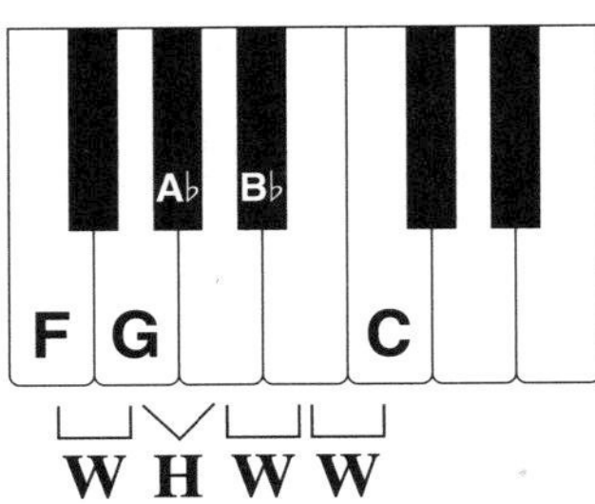

B♭ minor

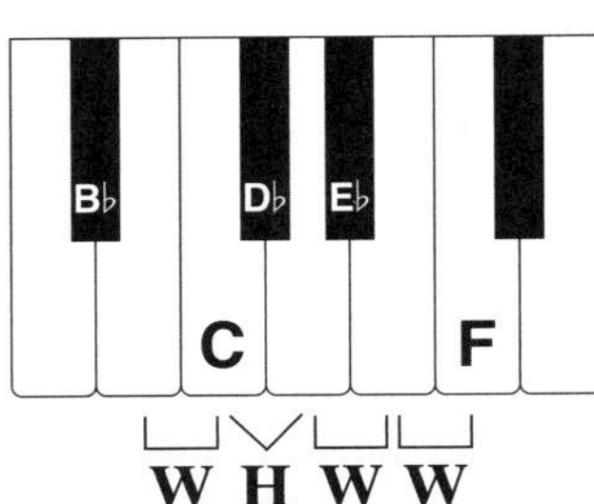

E♭ minor

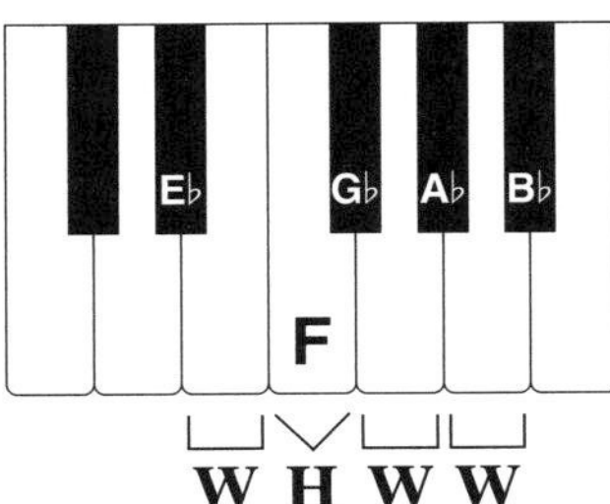

G♯ minor

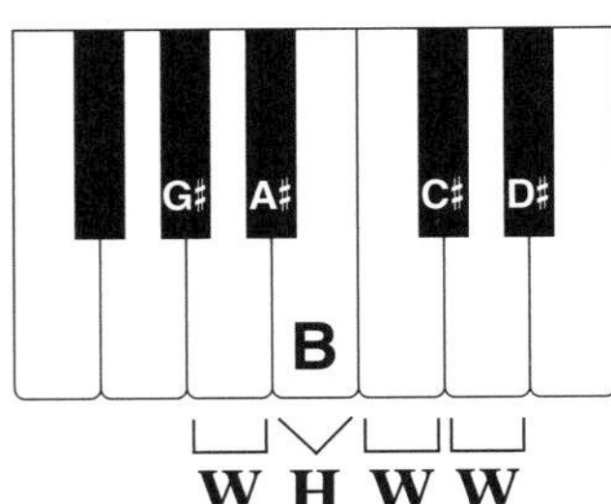

C♯ minor

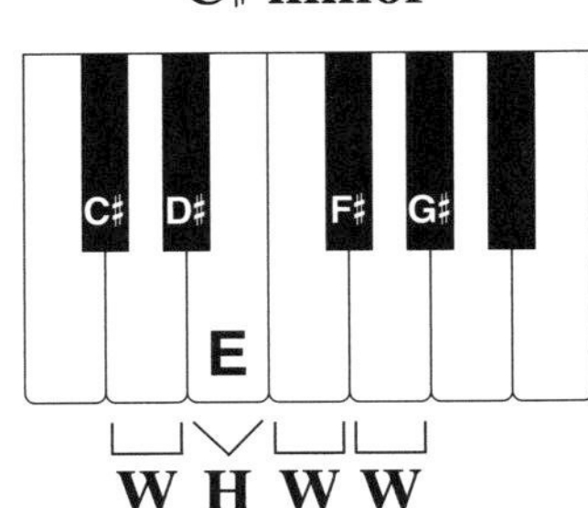

F♯ minor

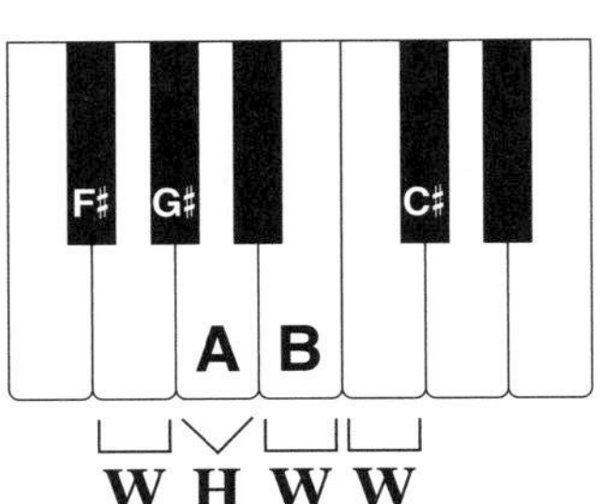

Your Turn!

Write the letter names of each minor 5-finger scale on the keyboard given.

Mark the **whole** steps, ⌴, and **half** steps, ∨, as shown on page 28.

C minor

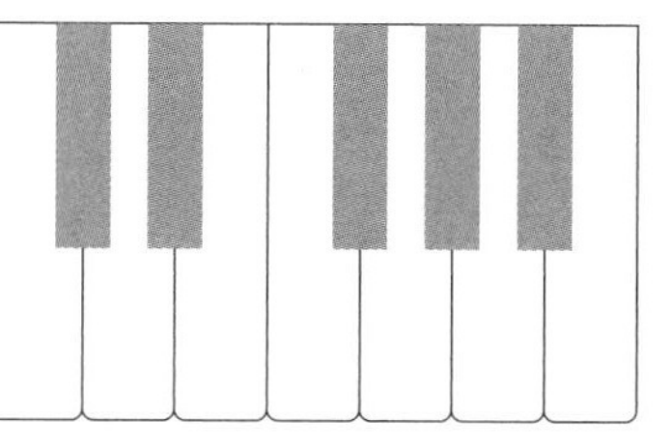

G minor

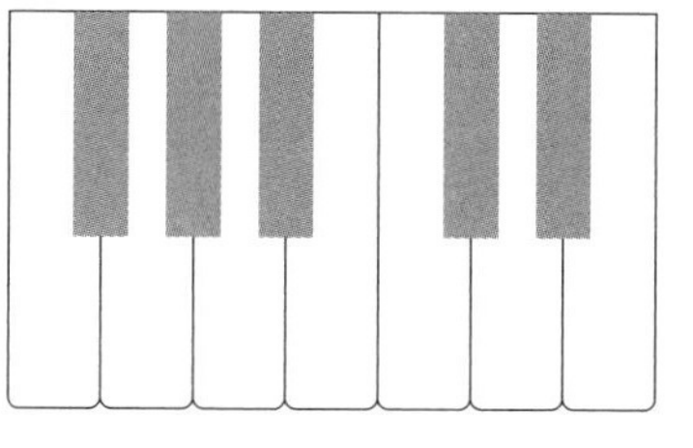

D minor

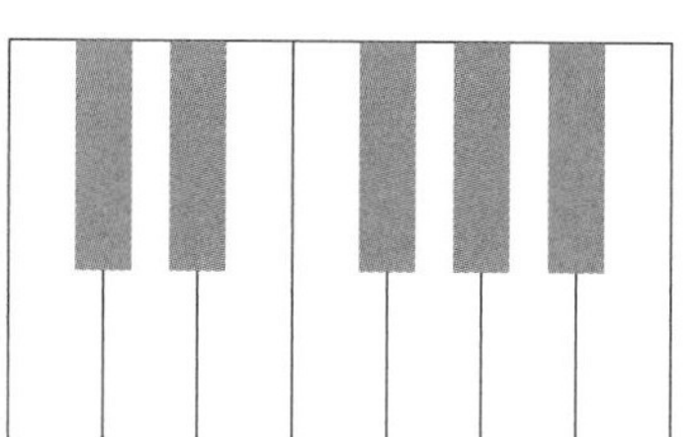

A minor

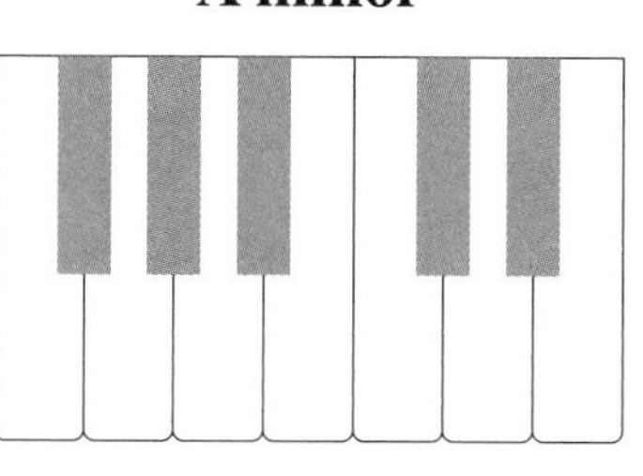
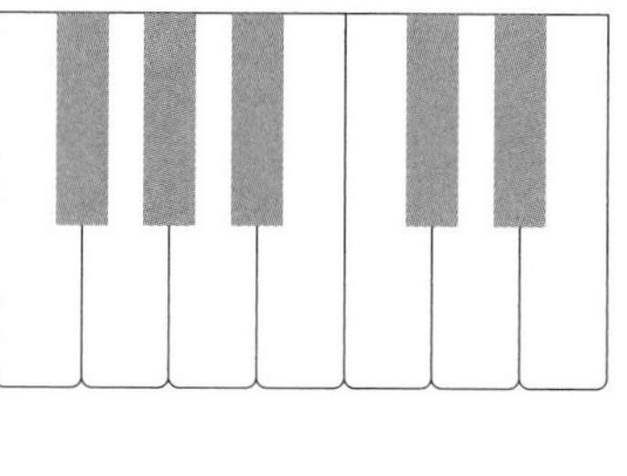
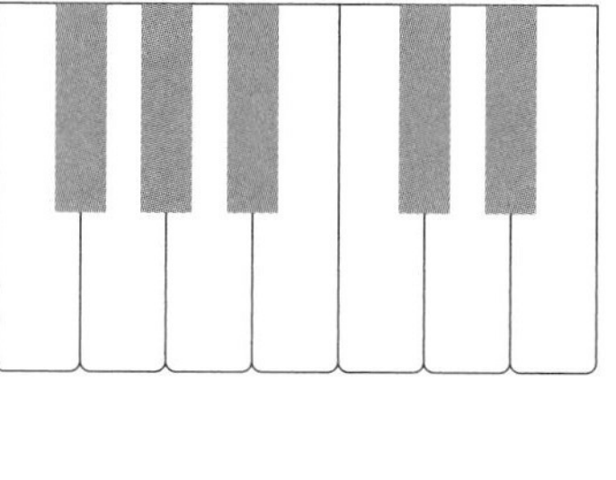

E minor

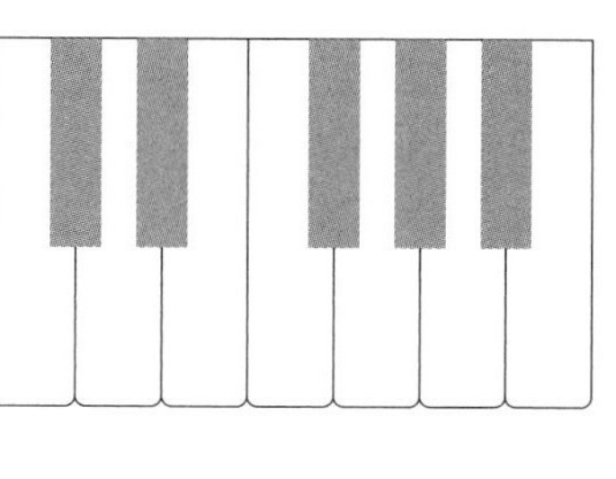

B minor

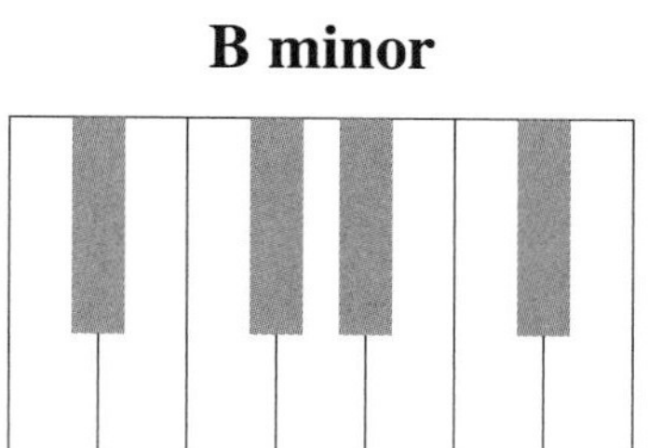
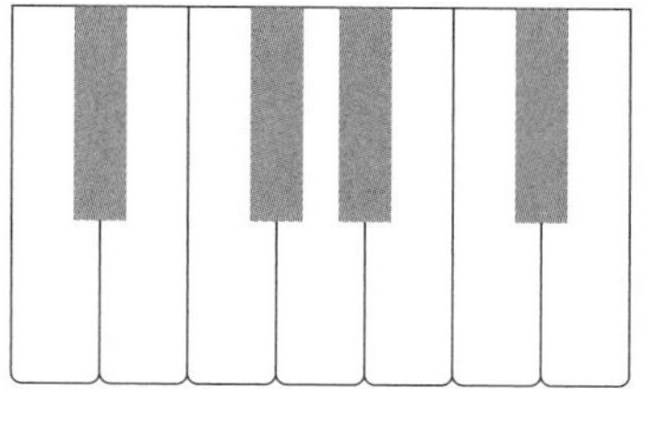

F minor

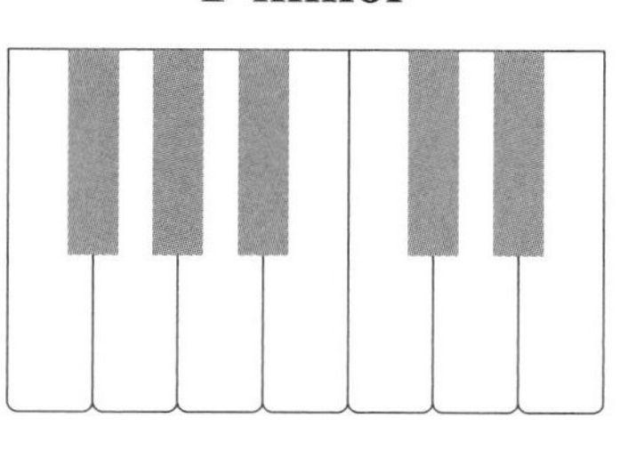

B♭ minor

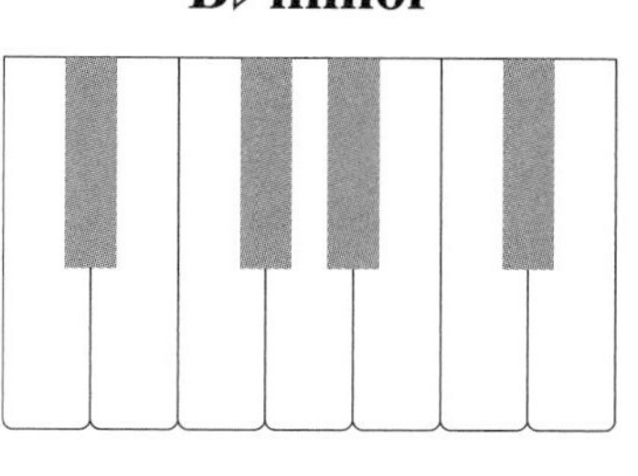

E♭ minor

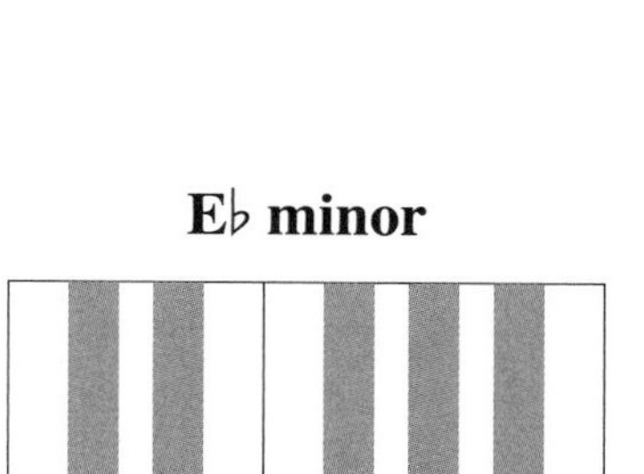

G♯ minor

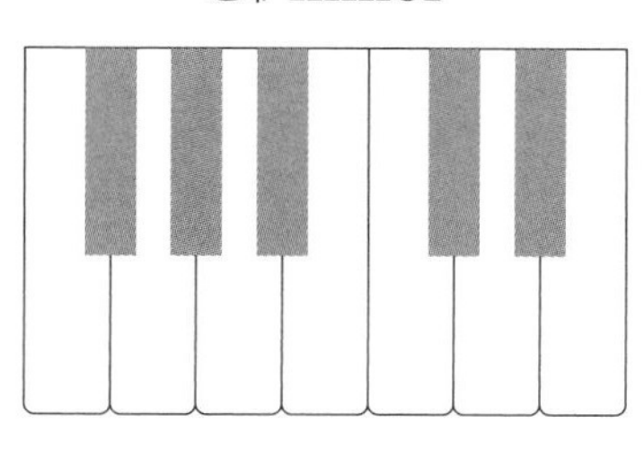

C♯ minor

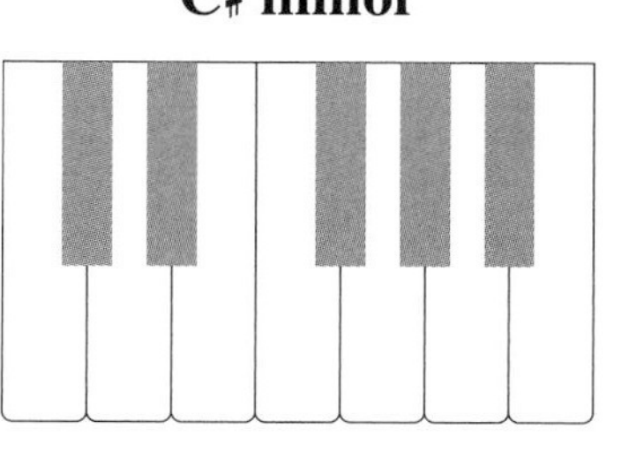

F♯ minor

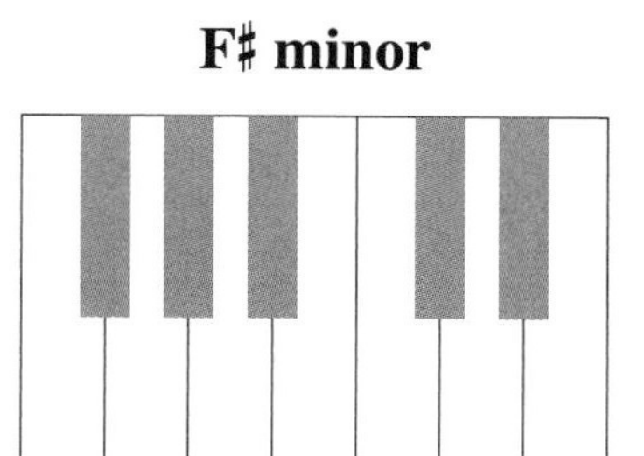

Minor Cross-Hand Arpeggios

After learning these well, your teacher may have you use the damper pedal.

A minor
f–p on repeat
L.H. over
E minor
f–p on repeat
L.H. over
B minor
f–p on repeat
L.H. over
Teacher Duets: (Student plays each exercise 1 octave higher)
R.H.
L.H.
mf–pp with pedal
R.H.
L.H.
mf–pp with pedal
R.H.
L.H.
mf–pp with pedal

F minor

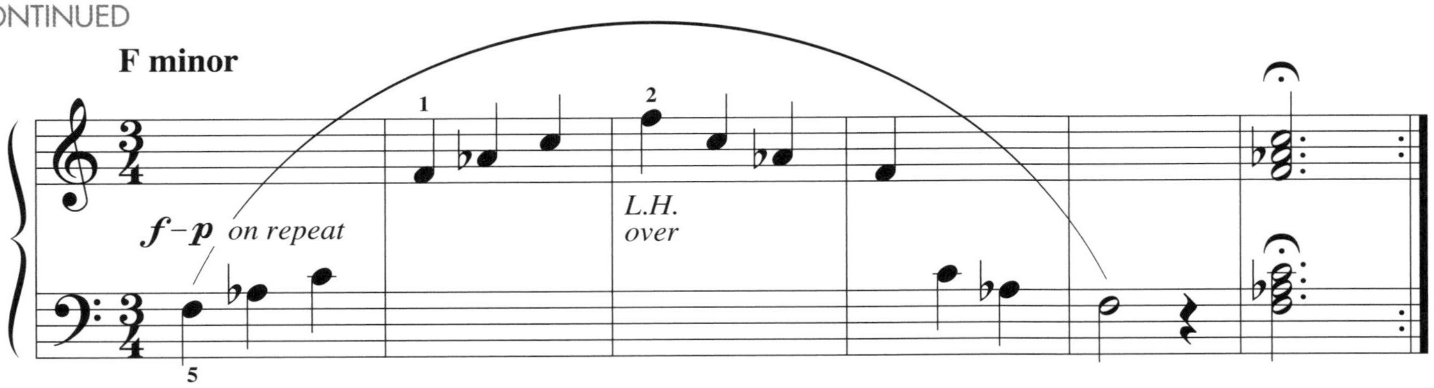

B♭ minor

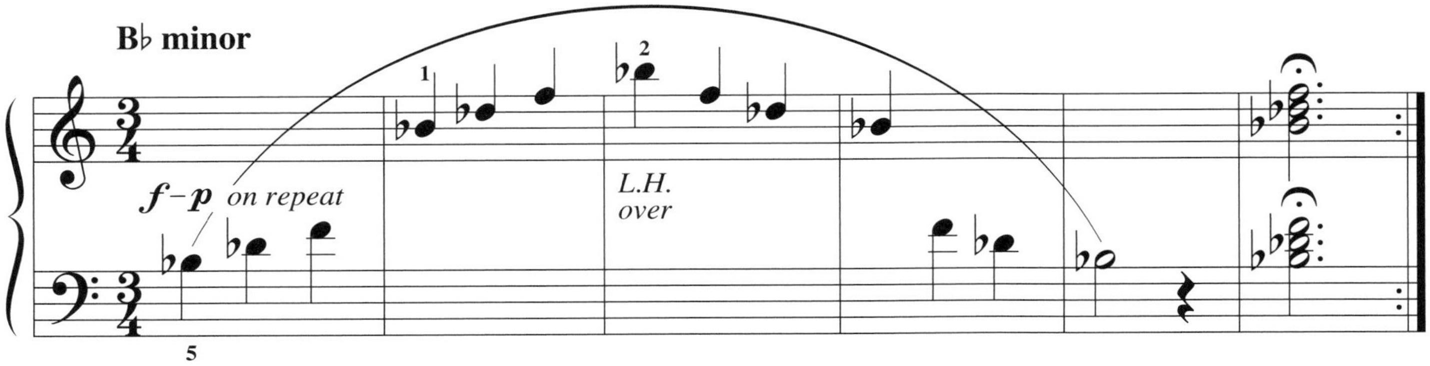

E♭ minor

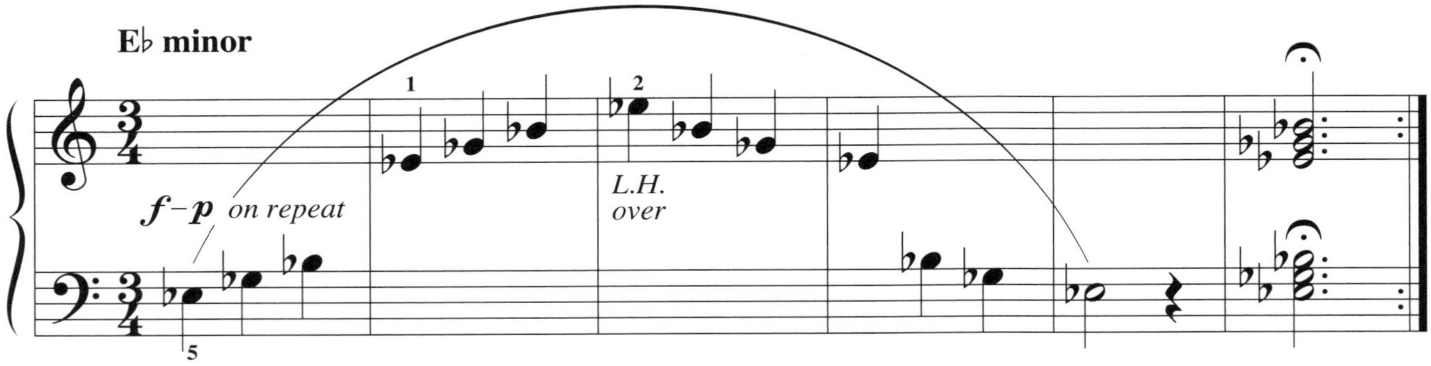

Teacher Duets: (Student plays each exercise *1 octave higher*)

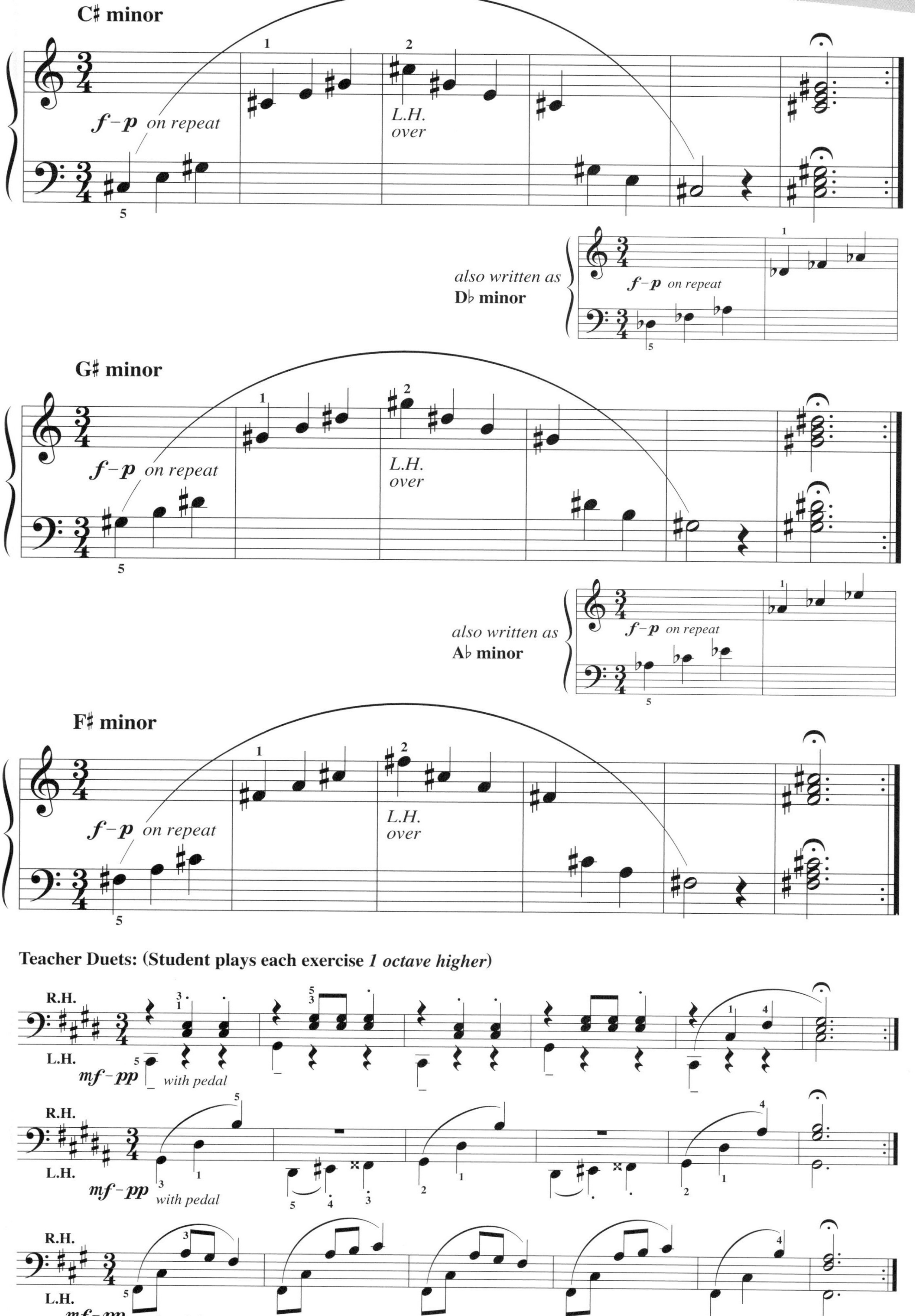
C♯ minor
1
2
f–p on repeat
L.H.
over
5
also written as
D♭ minor
f–p on repeat
1
5
G♯ minor
1
2
f–p on repeat
L.H.
over
5
also written as
A♭ minor
f–p on repeat
1
5
F♯ minor
1
2
f–p on repeat
L.H.
over
5
Teacher Duets: (Student plays each exercise 1 octave higher)
R.H.
L.H.
mf–pp with pedal
R.H.
L.H.
mf–pp with pedal
R.H.
L.H.
mf–pp with pedal

Jazzy Dance

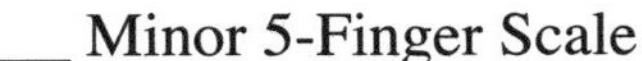

___ Minor 5-Finger Scale

Nancy Faber
(b. 1955)

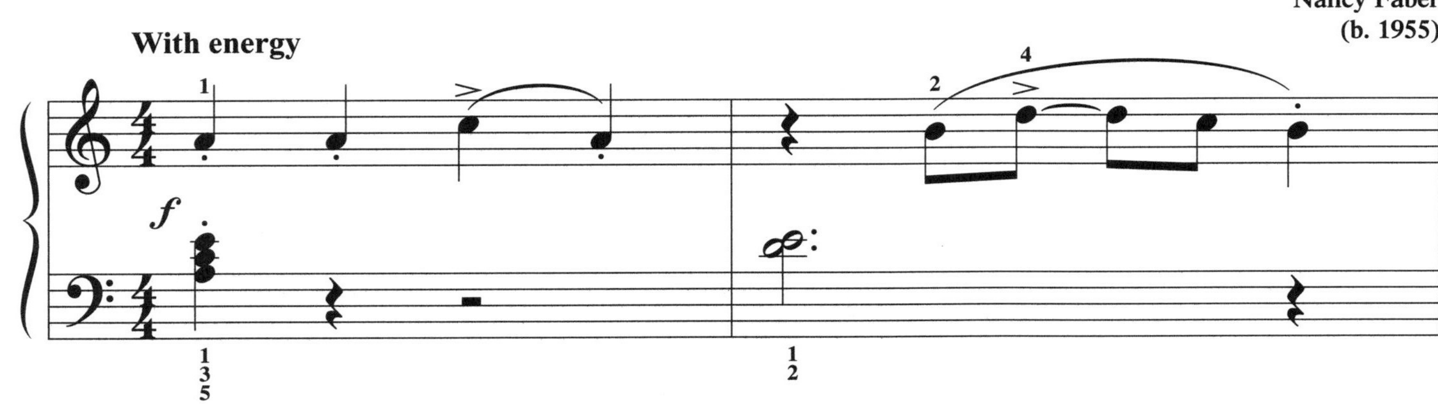

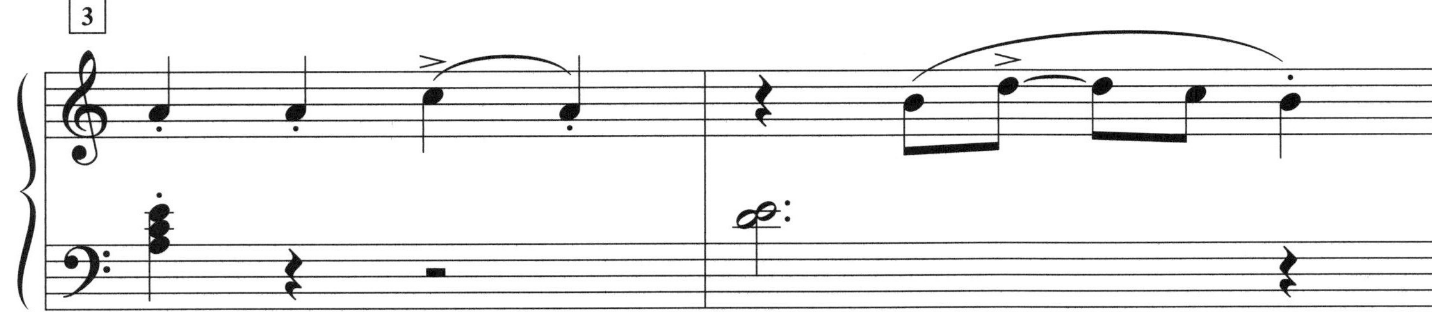

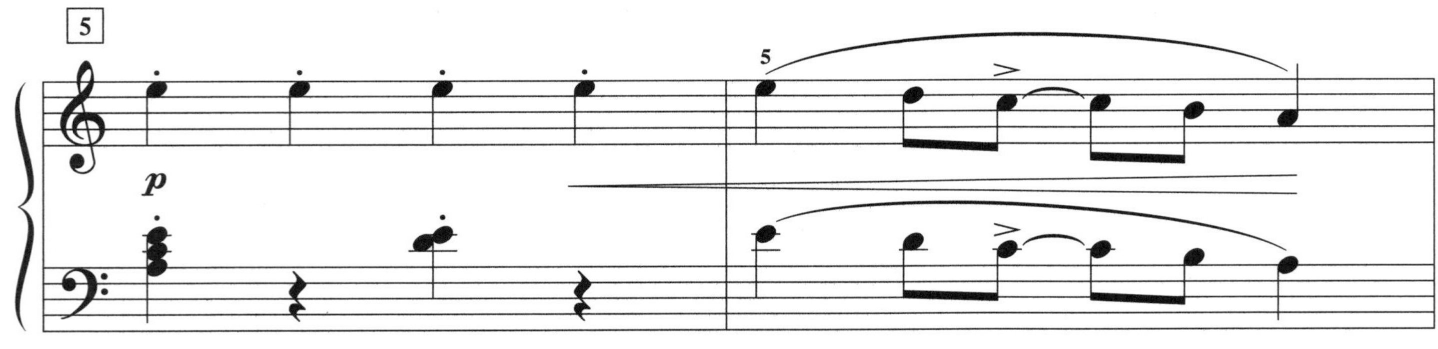

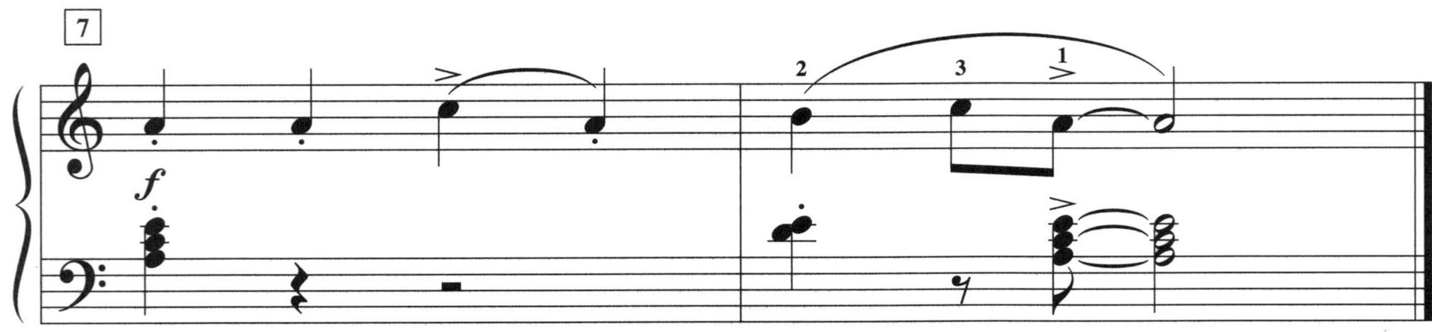

Cm	Gm	Dm	Am	Em	Bm	Fm	B♭m	E♭m	G♯m	C♯m	F♯m

Little March

Opus 300, No. 12*

___ Minor 5-Finger Scale

Louis Köhler
(1820–1886)

Cm	Gm	Dm	Am	Em	Bm	Fm	B♭m	E♭m	G♯m	C♯m	F♯m

Little Dance

from 24 Short and Easy Pieces*

___ Minor 5-Finger Scale

Alexander Reinagle
(1756–1809)
excerpt

Cm	Gm	Dm	Am	Em	Bm	Fm	B♭m	E♭m	G♯m	C♯m	F♯m

*Originally in C major.

Cadences in 12 Major Keys

I-V-I and I-V7-I Cadences

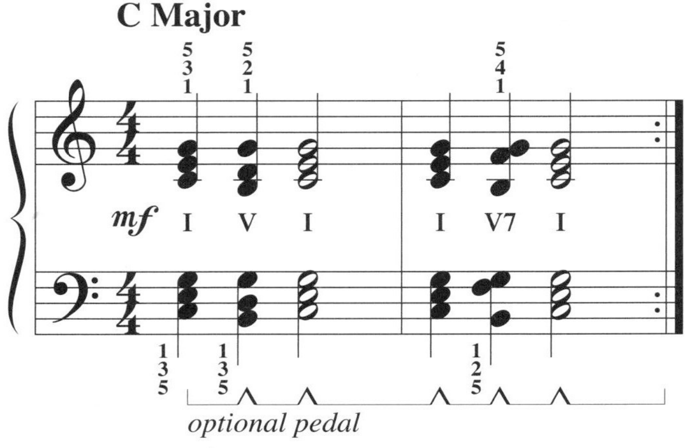

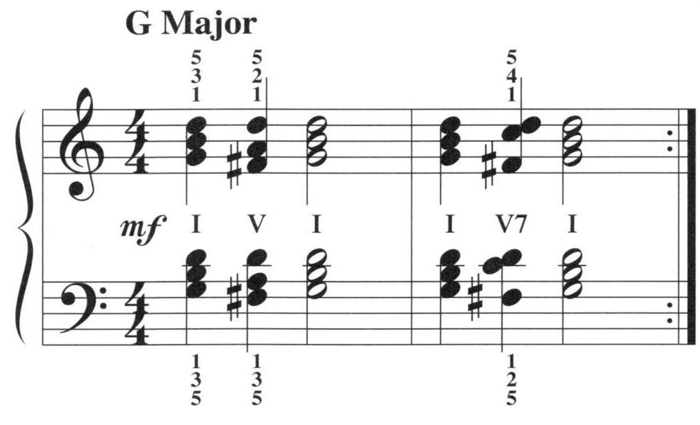

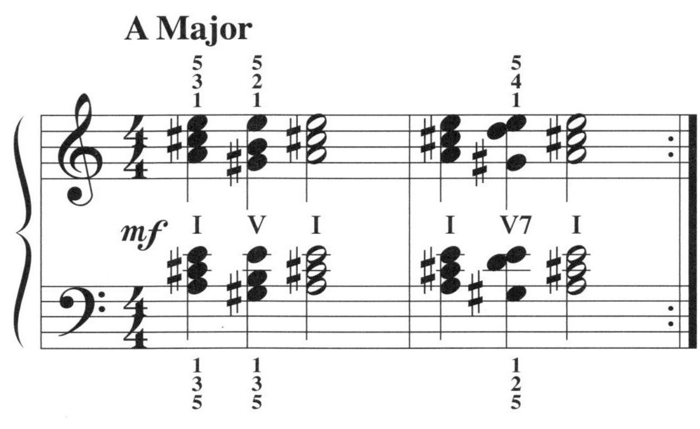

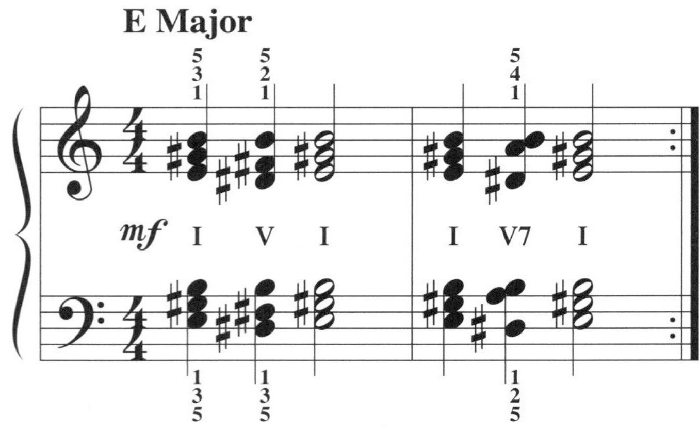

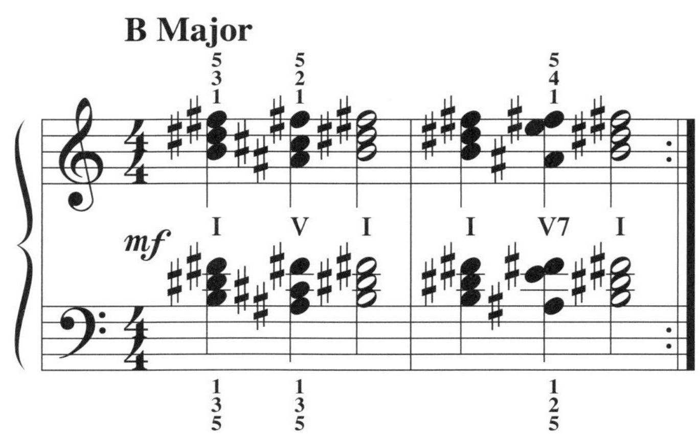

F Major

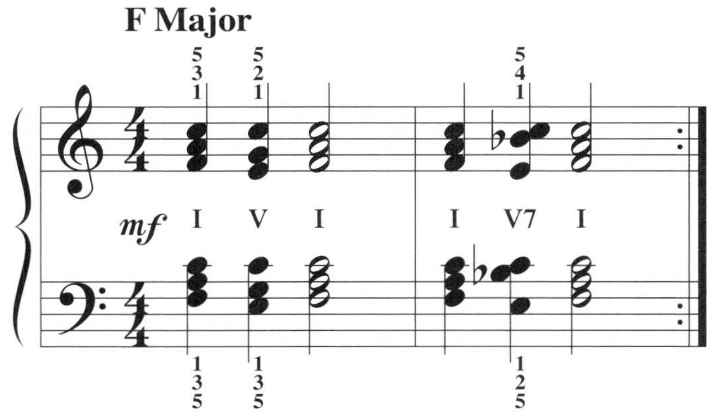

B♭ Major

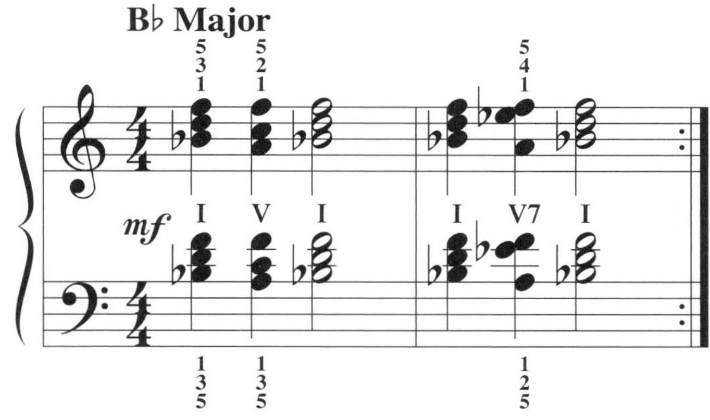

E♭ Major

A♭ Major

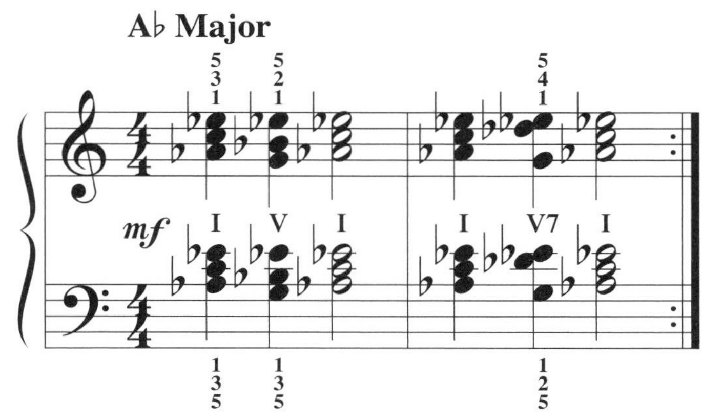

D♭ Major

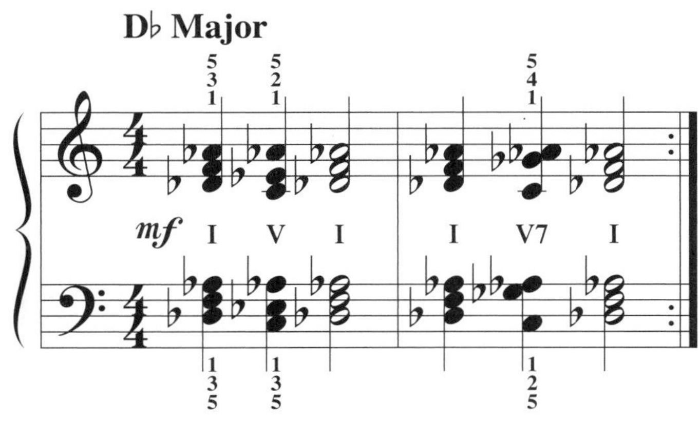

G♭ Major

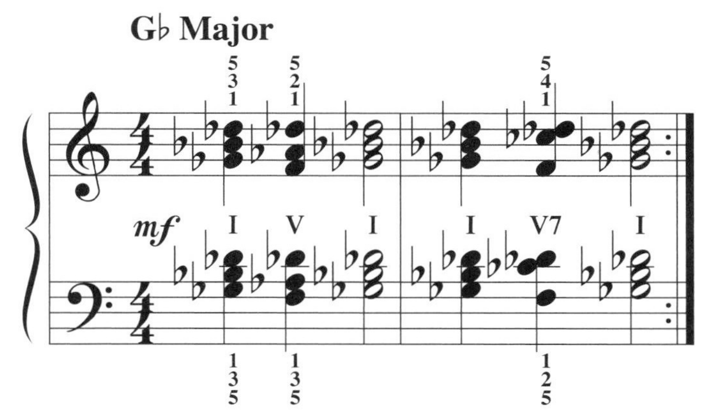

also written as

F♯ Major

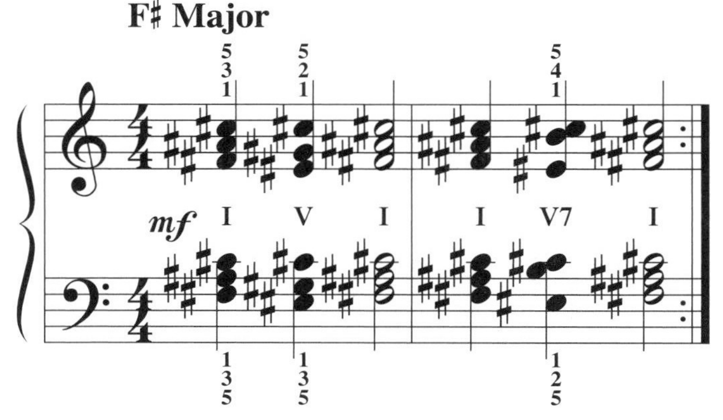

I-IV-I-V7-I Cadences

For this set of cadences, key signatures are used.

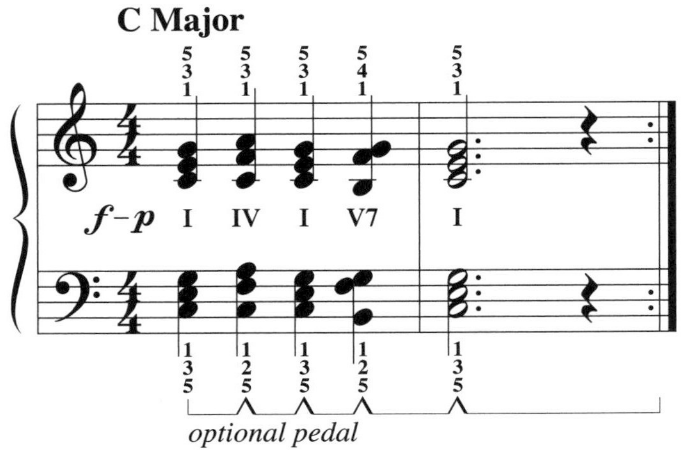

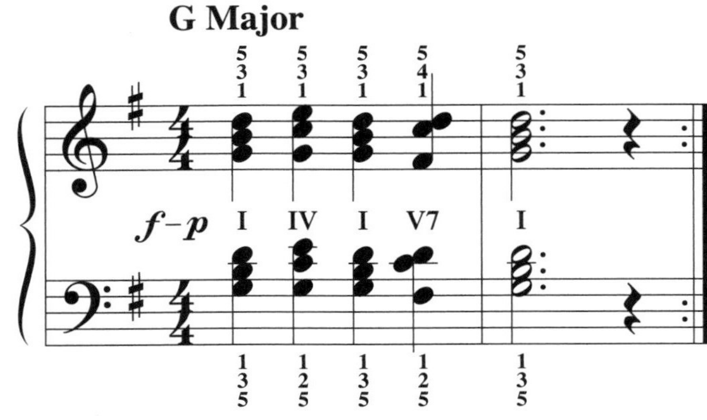

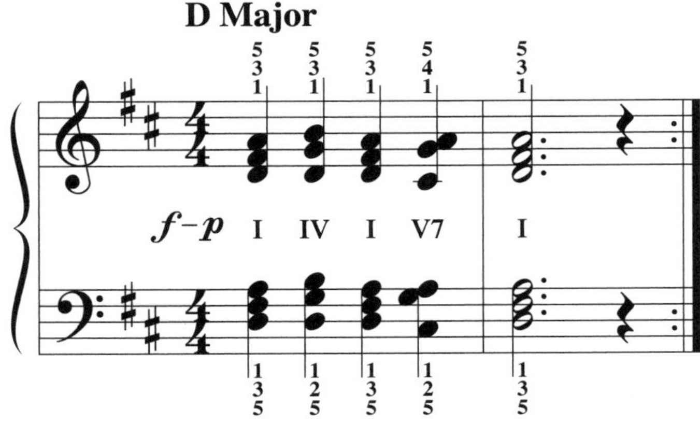

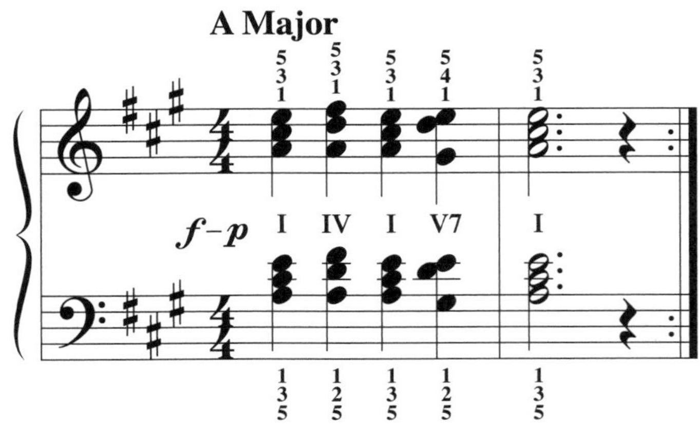

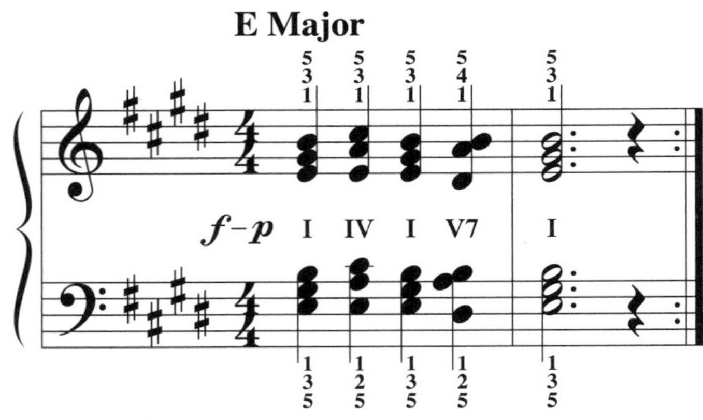

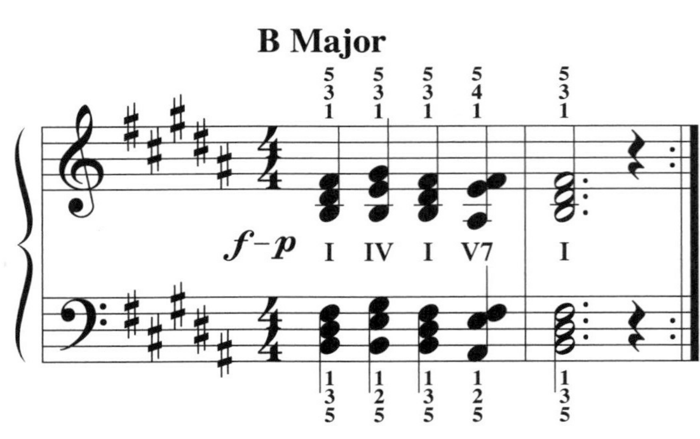

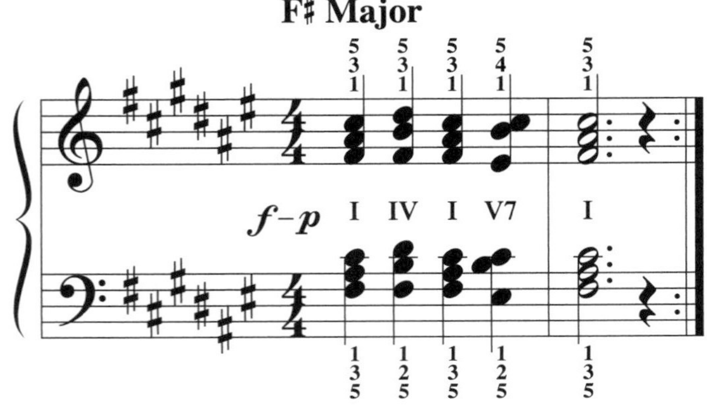

(also written as G♭ Major, page 39)

F Major

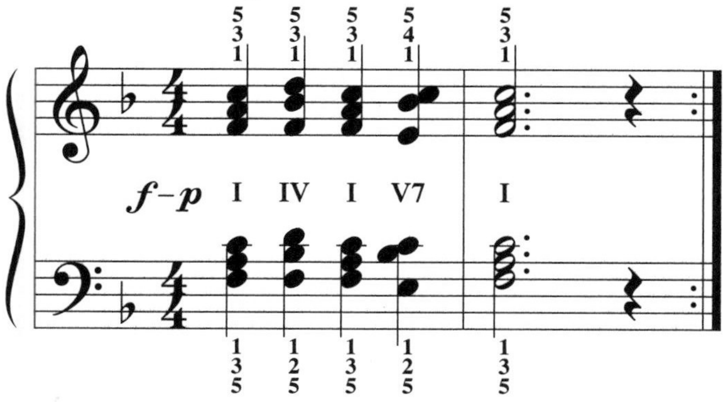

f–p I IV I V7 I

B♭ Major

f–p I IV I V7 I

E♭ Major

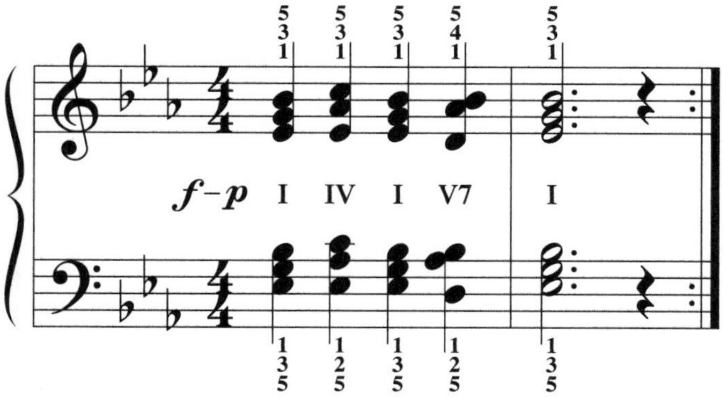

f–p I IV I V7 I

A♭ Major

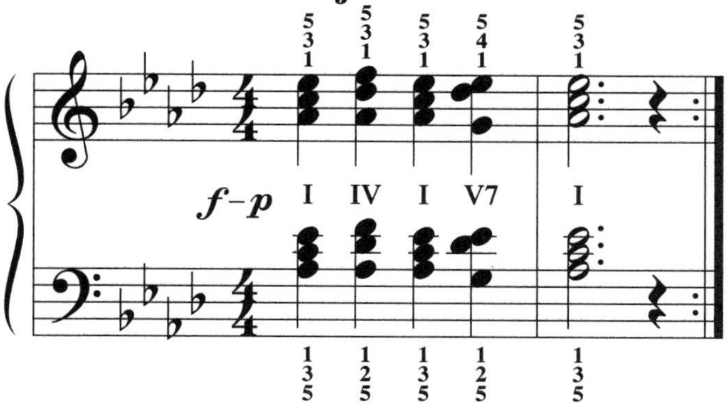

f–p I IV I V7 I

D♭ Major

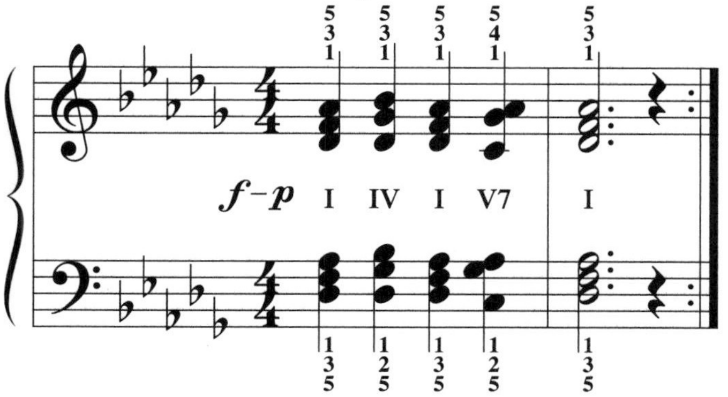

f–p I IV I V7 I

G♭ Major

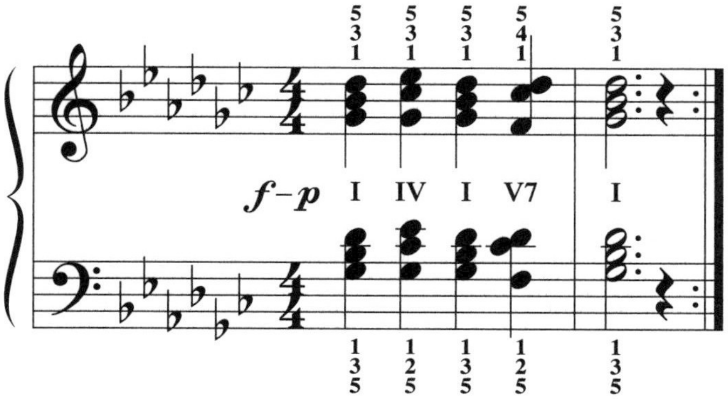

f–p I IV I V7 I

You may also practice the I-IV-I-V7-I cadences with roots in the bass, as follows:

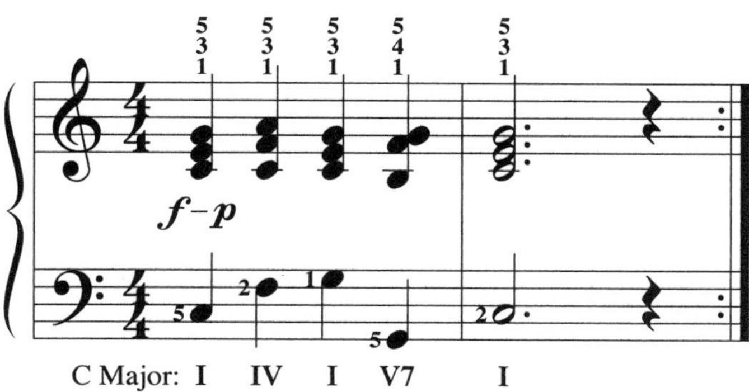

SECTION 8 Transposing with Primary Chords

I-V7 Harmony

Allegretto

from Op. 777, No. 2*

Key of ___ Major

Carl Czerny
(1791–1857)
original form

Allegretto

C	G	D	A	E	B	F	B♭	E♭	A♭	D♭	F♯ G♭

I-V7 Harmony

Little Joke

from Op. 117, No. 7*

Key of ___ Major

Cornelius Gurlitt
(1820–1901)
harmonized

Playfully

C	G	D	A	E	B	F	B♭	E♭	A♭	D♭	F♯ G♭

* excerpt

In May*

Key of ___ Major

Franz Behr
(1837-1898)
harmonized

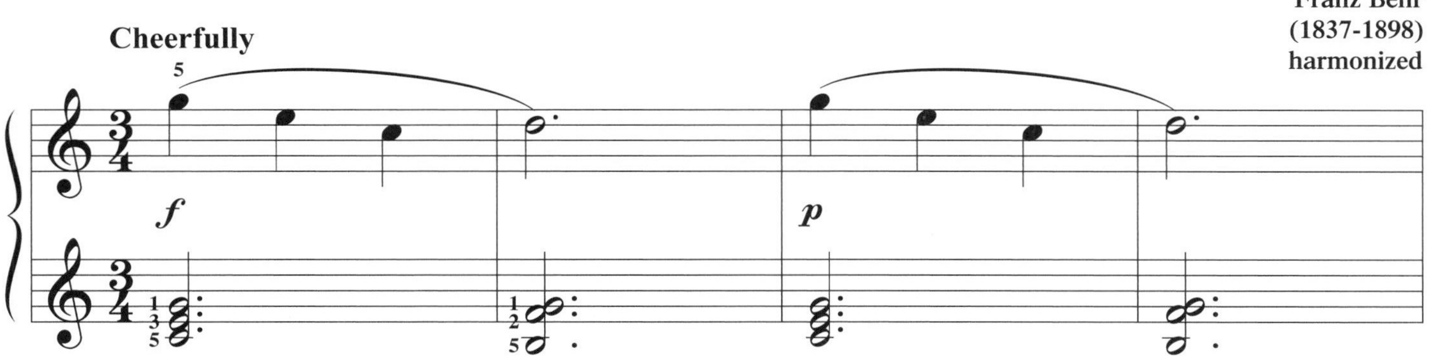

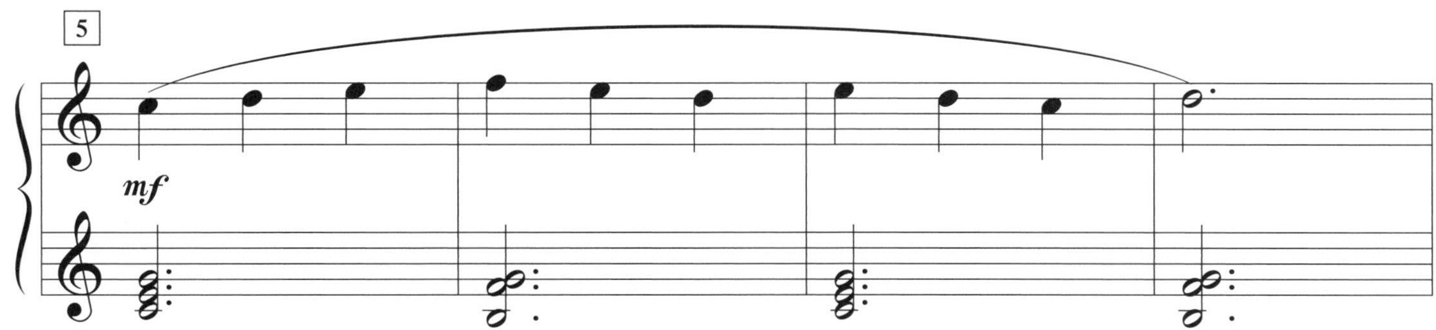

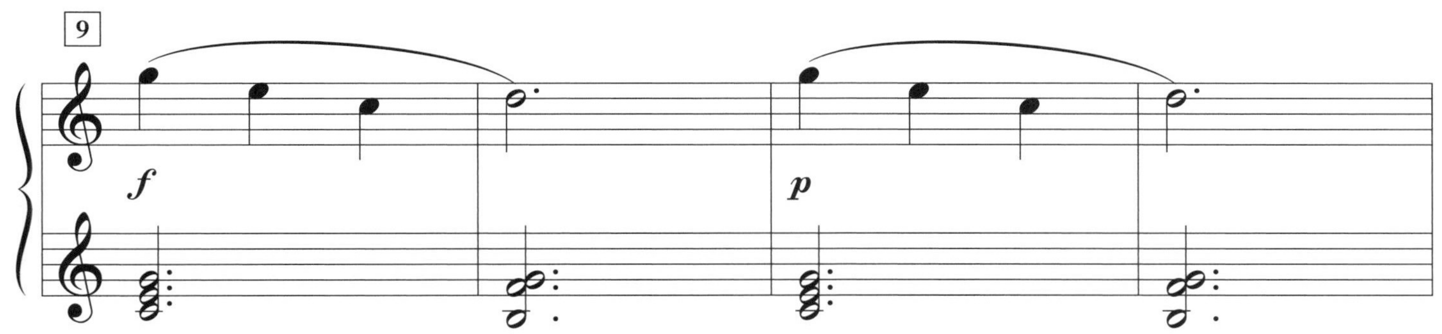

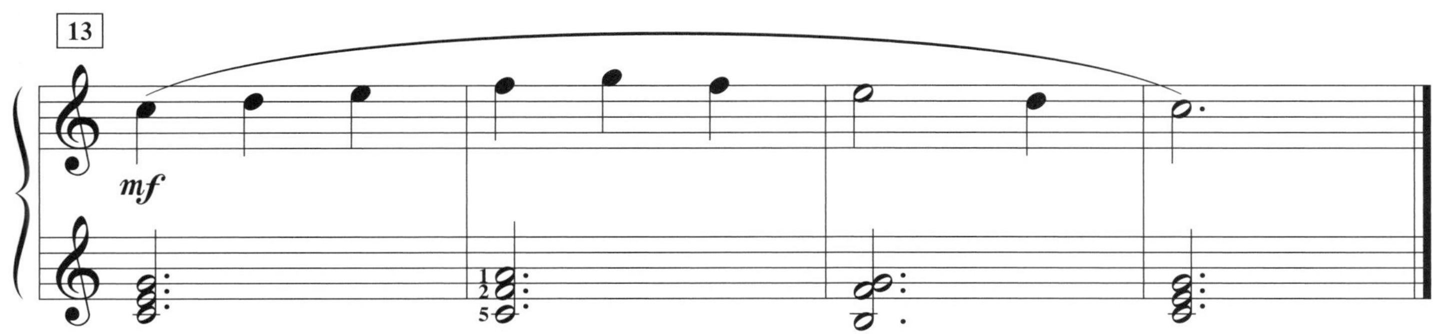

C	G	D	A	E	B	F	B♭	E♭	A♭	D♭	F♯ G♭

* excerpt

SECTION 9

Cadences in 12 Minor Keys

i-V-i and i-V7-i Cadences

C minor

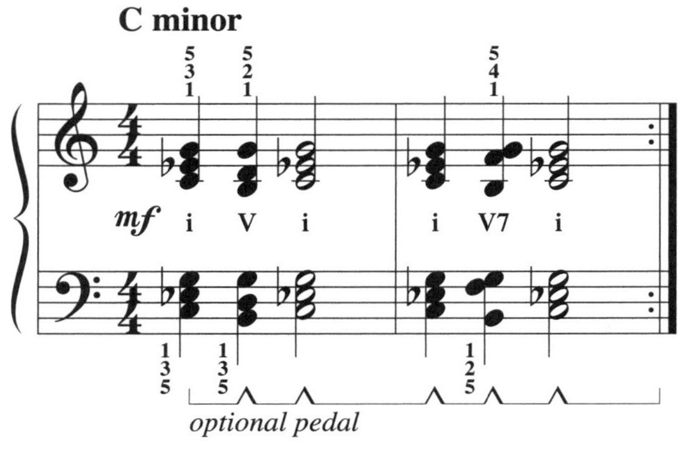

G minor

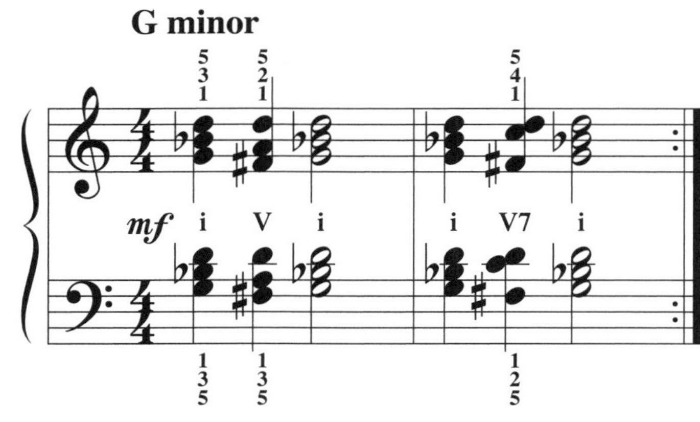

D minor

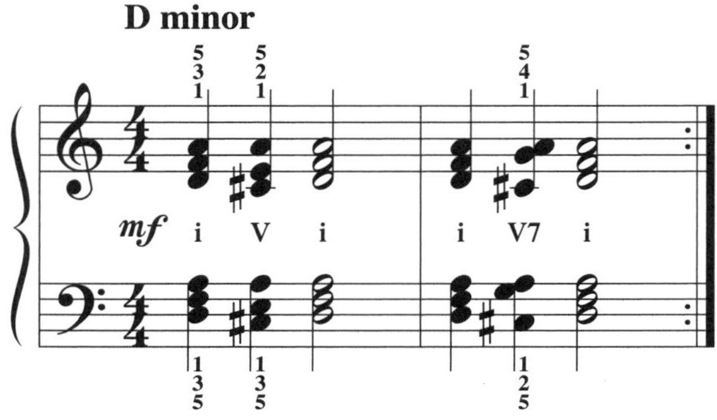

A minor

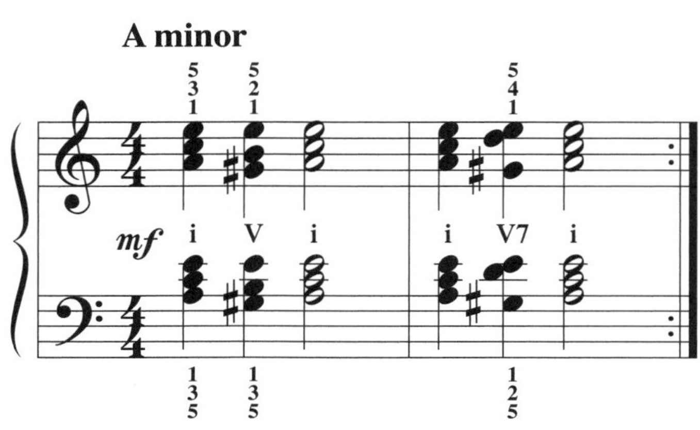

E minor

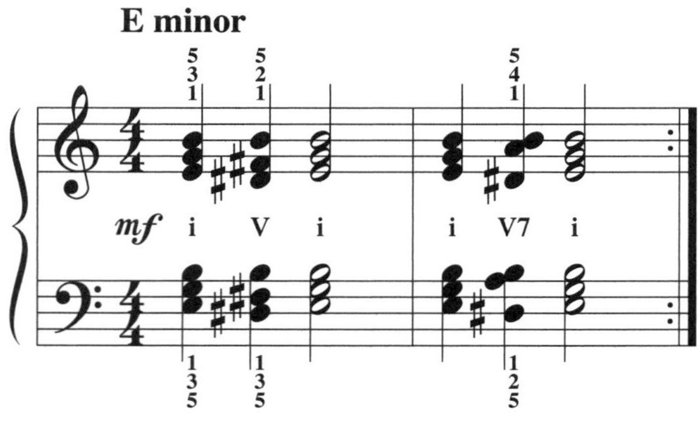

B minor

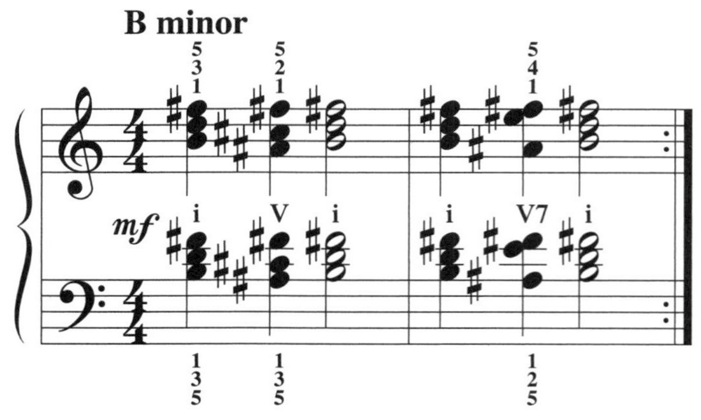

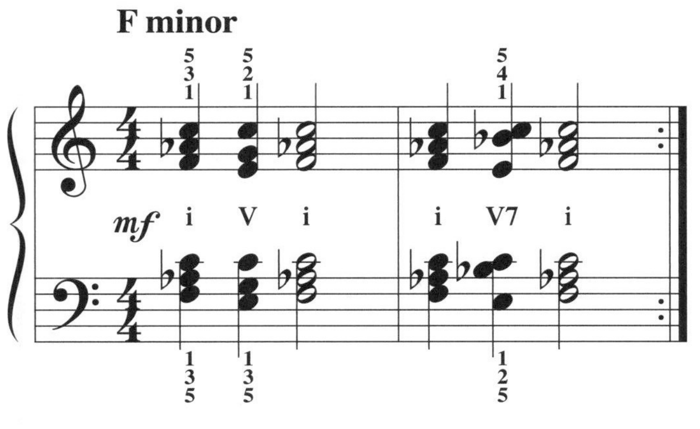

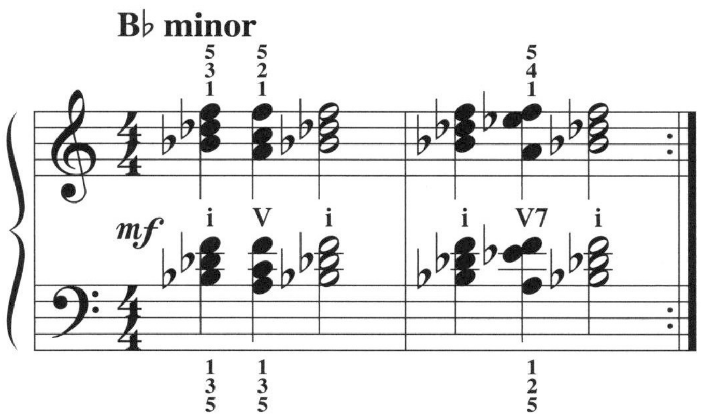

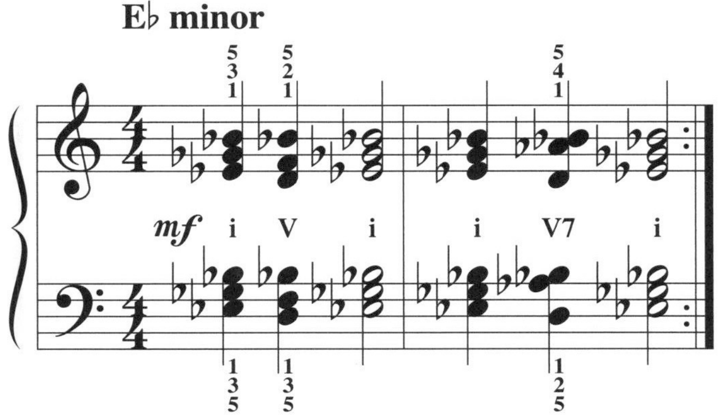

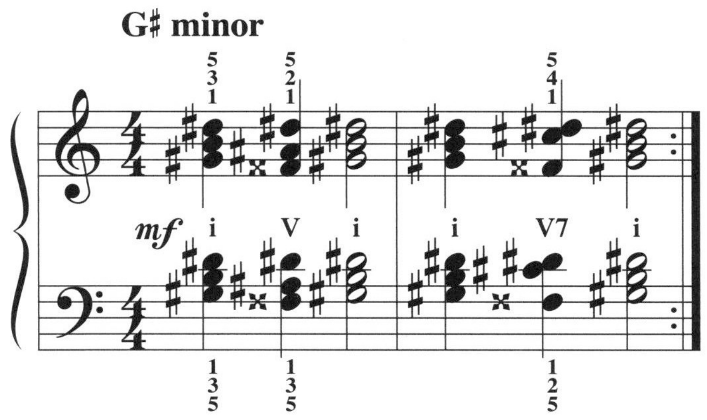

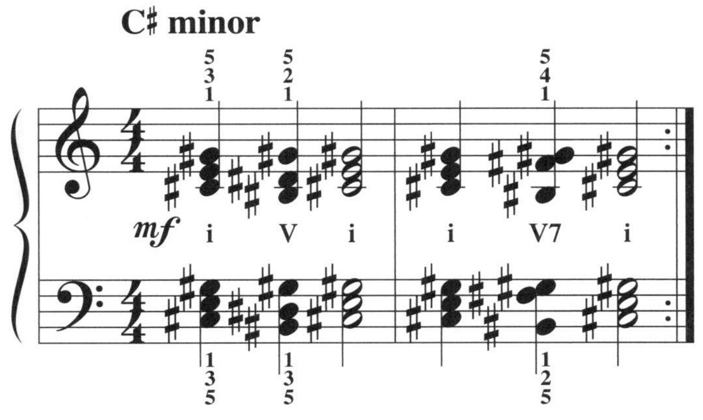

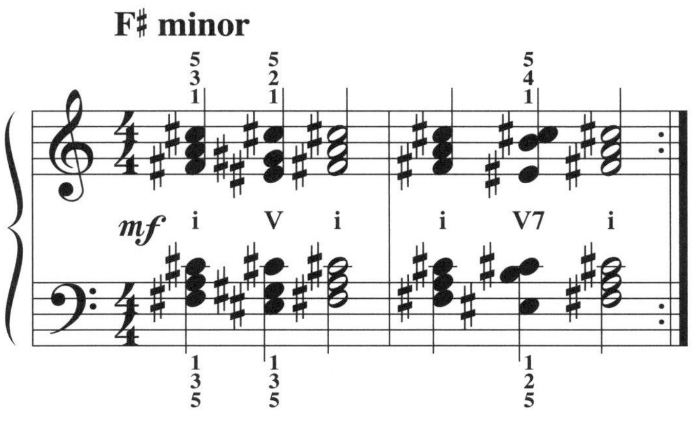

You may also practice the i-V-i cadences with roots in the bass, as follows:

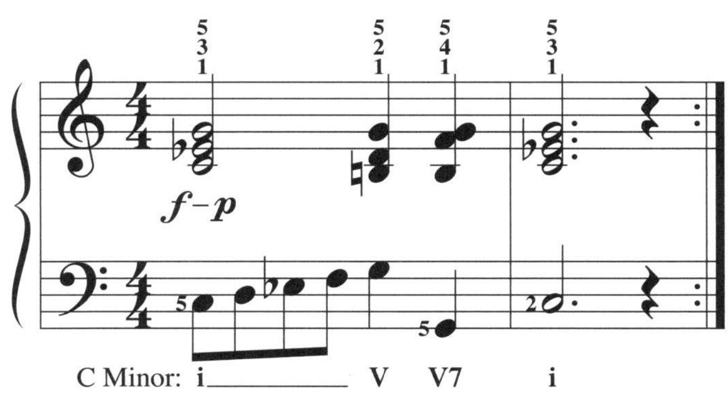

i-iv-i-V7-i Cadences

For this set of cadences, key signatures are used.

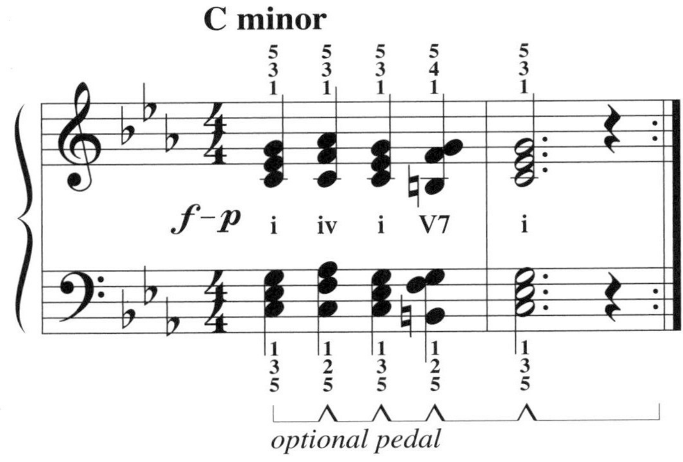

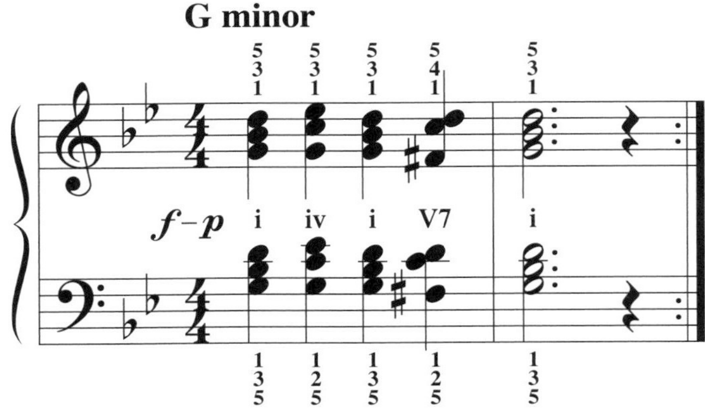

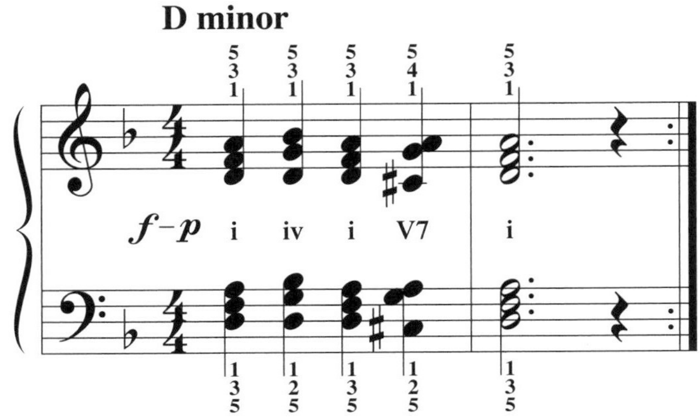

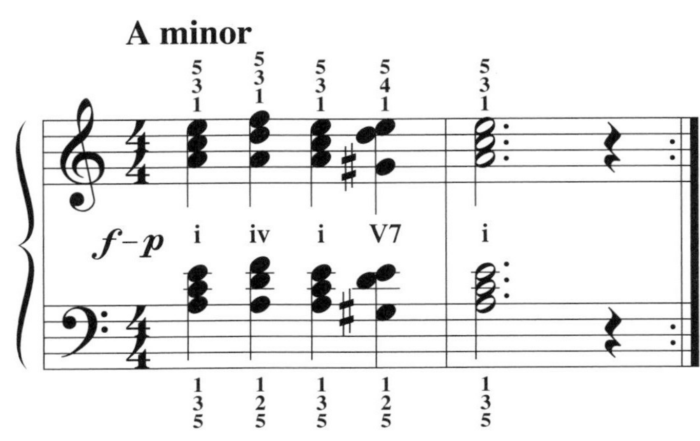

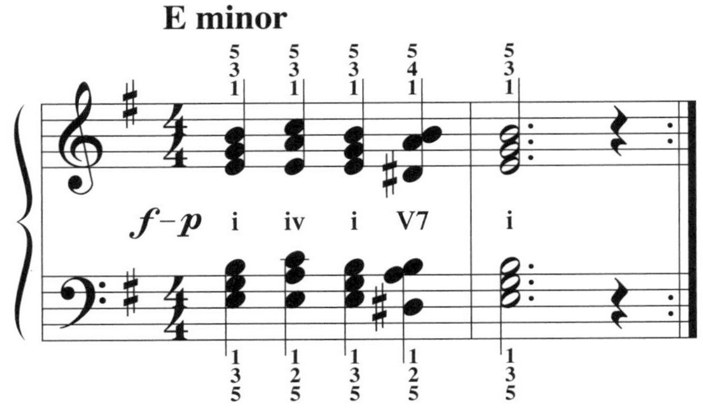

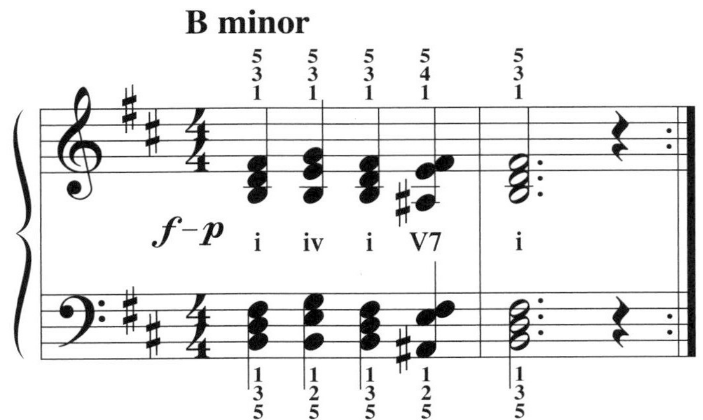

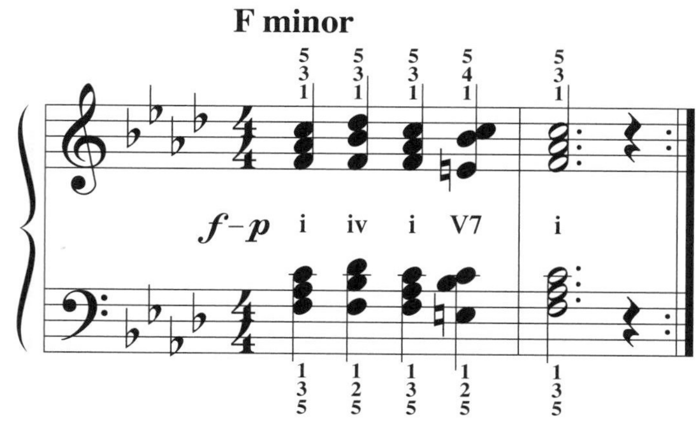
F minor
f–p
i iv i V7 i

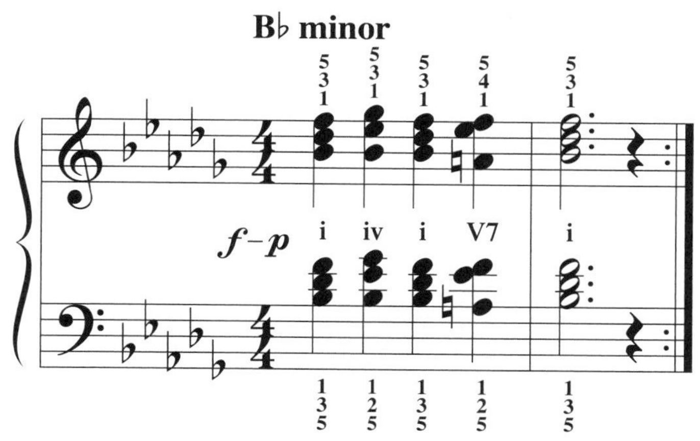
B♭ minor
f–p
i iv i V7 i

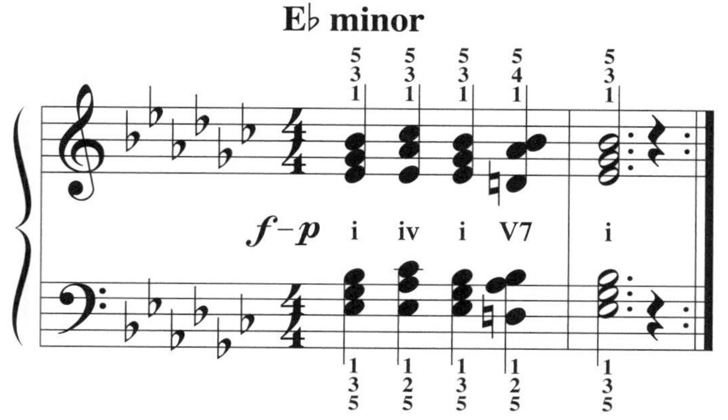
E♭ minor
f–p
i iv i V7 i

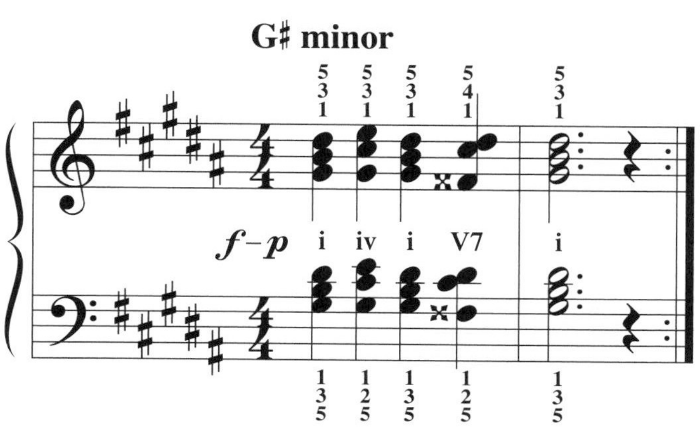
G♯ minor
f–p
i iv i V7 i

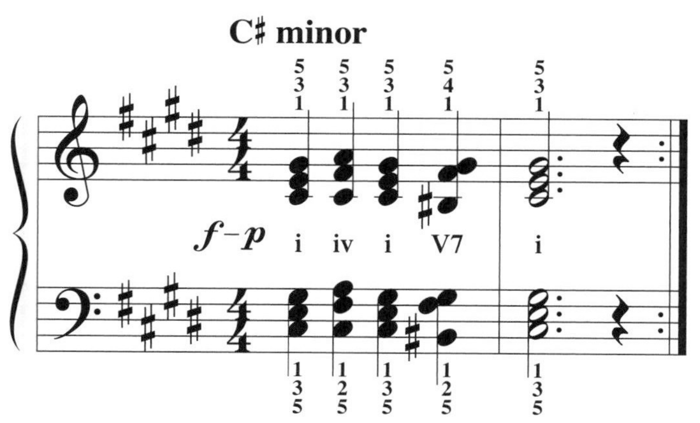
C♯ minor
f–p
i iv i V7 i

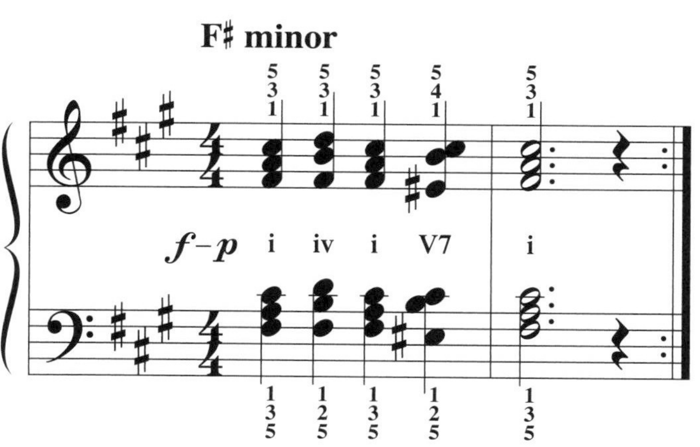
F♯ minor
f–p
i iv i V7 i

SECTION 10

Transposing with Primary Chords

Little March

i-V7 Harmony

Key of ___ Minor*

Daniel Gottlob Türk
(1750-1813)
harmonized

Andante

mp

Cm	Gm	Dm	Am	Em	Bm	Fm	B♭m	E♭m	G♯m	C♯m	F♯m

Allegro

i-V7 Harmony

from First Instruction in Piano-playing, No. 5*

Key of ___ Minor

Carl Czerny
(1791–1857)
harmonized, excerpt

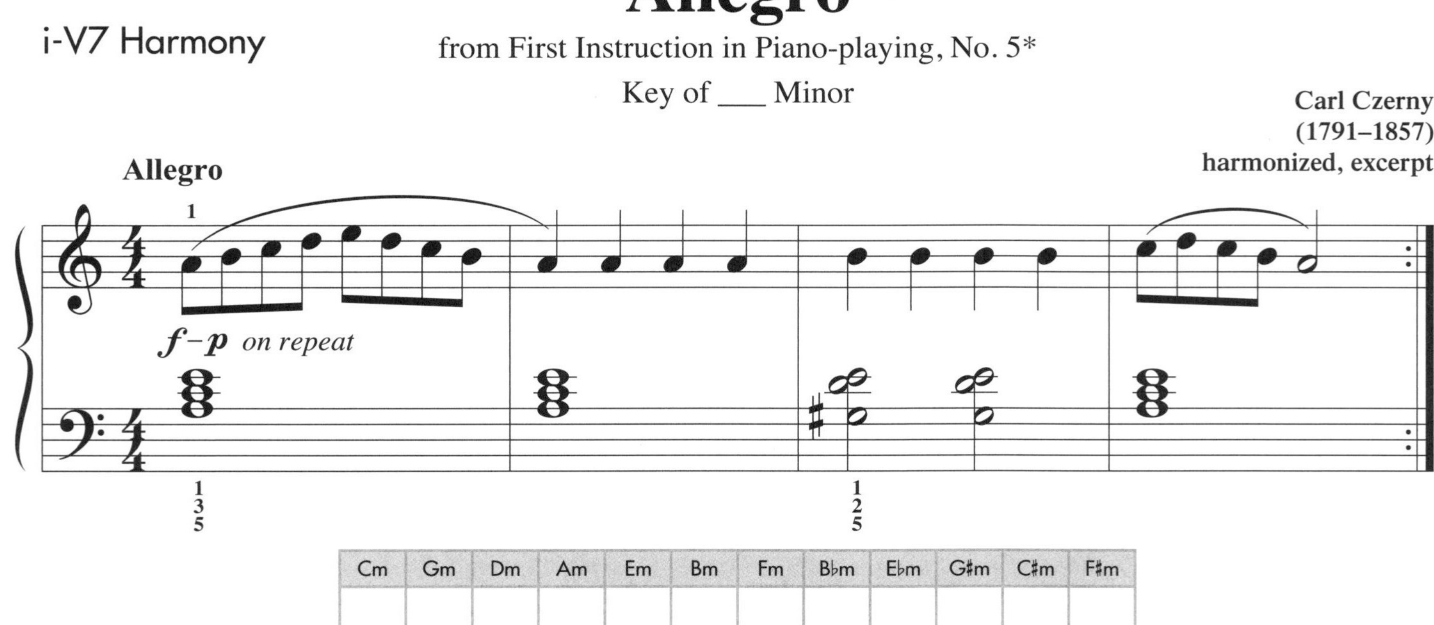

Cm	Gm	Dm	Am	Em	Bm	Fm	B♭m	E♭m	G♯m	C♯m	F♯m

*Originally in C major.

The Troll's March

i-iv-V7 Harmony

from Op. 149, No. 3*

Key of ___ Minor

Anton Diabelli
(1781-1858)
harmonized

Moderato

f

5

9

p

Cm	Gm	Dm	Am	Em	Bm	Fm	B♭m	E♭m	G♯m	C♯m	F♯m

*Originally in C major for Four Hands. Excerpted from the Primo part.

Certificate of Achievement

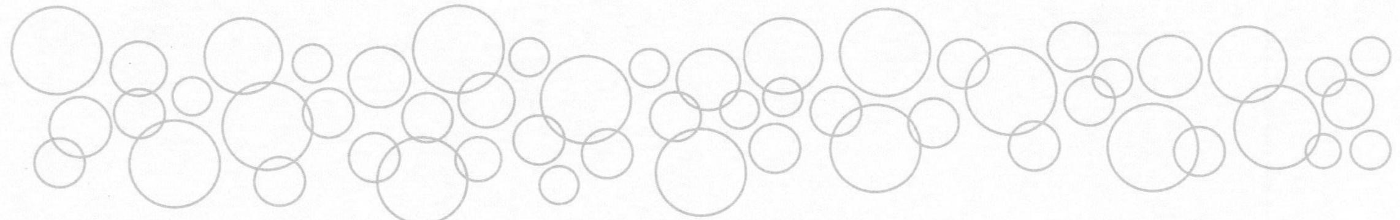

CONGRATULATIONS TO

____

You have completed

PIANO ADVENTURES® SCALE BOOK 1

You are now ready for

PIANO ADVENTURES® SCALE BOOK 2

Keep up the good work!

____
Teacher

____
Date